B

DESTINY UNKNOWN

DESTINY UNKNOWN

by

Derek Leinster

Magna Large Print Books
Long Preston, North Yorkshire,
BD23 4ND, England.

British Library Cataloguing in Publication Data.

Leinster, Derek
    Destiny unknown.

    A catalogue record of this book is
    available from the British Library

    ISBN   978-0-7505-3439-0

First published in Great Britain in 2008 by
Derek Leinster

Copyright © Derek Leinster

Cover illustration © David Ridley by arrangement with
Arcangel Images

The moral right of the author has been asserted.

Published in Large Print 2011 by arrangement with
Derek Linster

Magna Large Print is an imprint of Library Magna Books Ltd.

Printed and bound in Great Britain by
T.J. (International) Ltd., Cornwall, PL28 8RW

This book is based on my honest recollections from my own life.

Some of the names have been changed to protect some people.

Acknowledgements

I've written this book with lots of help from Bernice Walmsley and would like to thank her for her hard work, her creative input and efficient organisation.

I'd also like to thank other people who helped me to realise the dream of writing this second book about my life – Betty, Monica at the Arts Council, students at the Bishop Pronian School, Worcester who helped to design the cover, Princethorpe College, Paul Hubbard, Sarah Hackett, Simon McCarthy (Coventry Outreach Society), Charles Gallagher and the many others, too numerous to mention, who have made a valuable, and valued, contribution in the process of bringing this book together.

Above all, I must thank my wife, Carol, for putting up with hearing about this story continuously over many, many years and my four daughters – Debbie, Amanda, Gail and Kerry – who have also had to endure this marathon.

Derek Leinster 2008

Home At Last!

The journey was long but now I'm here
England I'm excited with fear.
So many new faces
Loads of new rules
I won't need to ride up on the mules.
I met a family hooray for me
The shock was like being stung by a bee
How did I do it?
How did I feel?
Read this book it will tell you for real.

**Hannah Summers age 11
& Danielle Wilkins age 12**

Two of Derek Leinster's granddaughters

I miss you dear old Donegal

In Oxford England I was born
But raised in Ireland
In dear old Co. Donegal
Where the scenery's still grand.

But times were hard
In those far off days
For me mum, dad, sister & me
So me dad he left
To look for work
In a land across the sea.

We struggled on for a few more years
Through the good times and the bad
But soon me mum she left us too
To join up with me dad.

We were left with our grandparents
Who had a little farm
They brought us up
They cared for us
And kept us from all harm.

We had no running water
No carpets on the floor
We had no electricity
Just a paraffin lamp and its globe.

But we had our friends and neighbours
Who came round every night
To play a game of 25
In the paraffin's flickering light.

Many's a game was lost and won
And many's a song was sung
Around the old turf fire
Where on the crook the kettle hung.

But those were days of long ago
They'll ne'er be the same again
The old folk are all dead and gone
They young ones gone away.

The little house where I was raised
Yes, it's standing still
But now it's used for sheltering sheep
That come down from the hill.

So here I am in a foreign land
Far across the sea
But my love for Ireland and Donegal
Will always be with me.

I miss you dear old Donegal
For I am getting old
But I'm happy in this heart of mine
'Cos my thoughts of you I've told.

I miss you dear old Donegal
No matter where I roam
'Cos Upper Keeldrum, Gortahork
Will always be my home.

Yes, Upper Keeldrum, Gortahork
Will always be my home.

C Gallagher.

Introduction

My dreams of going to England started very early in my life. It always seemed to me that it must be a wonderful place. A place where dreams could come true and where I would be somebody. A place where I would not be ignored as I had been for the whole of my young life in rural Ireland. I often day-dreamed about a new life in England as I went about my chores around the house and out in the fields around my foster home in Dunganstown. Certainly by the time I was 14 years of age I had become obsessed with finding a way to get there.

I suppose, when you consider that I was an ignorant boy who had virtually no idea what going to England would entail, then my dreams about life in England were totally unrealistic, but understandable. I couldn't really imagine life there and the difficulties that it could hold for someone like me – although I constantly thought about it. In my ignorance. I would not have known that application forms needed to be filled in for jobs, for example. This was something that was totally unheard of in the little village where I lived. There you just heard about a job and asked if you could have it. Another thing I hadn't appreciated was that clocks on walls were certainly nothing to do with home decorations and that you would have to conform to being on time to fit into this new society and what it demanded of you. I did not have a clock or a watch to go by so, as a child, all of this would have been a totally different ball game and one that I would not have even thought of.

So, why would a boy of 14 years old be so fired up with the desire to leave the beautiful country of Ireland for other pastures, when none of these questions had been answered? I suppose you have got to put it down to one thing – my ignorance. Remember that there was no TV or radio in my life to show me the world outside my little community. There were no daily newspapers – and even if there had been they would not have meant a lot as I was unable to read. Then you have to dig deeper to know the truth about my situation. You see, in the 1940s and 50s in Southern Ireland the majority of people you would meet as a boy were either going to England or were back on holiday from England, and at that age you would probably think that this was a bit of excitement, a new adventure. It most certainly was an adventure for me but, believe me, I would have had more control of my adventure if I had been properly educated. If I am honest I would have to accept that, because of my oppressed boyhood and youth, part of my brain would not have developed to more than that of a 12 year old even at that stage of my life as I prepared to go to England at the age of 18. I was a young man, of course, but I had no more understanding of the world than a boy. The odd thing is you have no idea at the time that that is the case. It is only when you go further on up the road, getting a bit of experience of life, that you find you have not had the same advantages as other people have had. I suppose setting out to follow a dream to emigrate to England is not a good idea when you are embarking on such a journey so badly equipped to take on this new world. I was about to dice with destiny, and when you are dealing with destiny at 18 years of age you just have no idea where that destiny may take you. In my life in Ireland I had no real way of finding out the truth about life in England – I would just have to follow my dream and meet my destiny, whatever it was.

One crisp February Sunday morning in 1960, after church, I called in to see my foster father as usual and he told me that he had made contact with Molly, his daughter who already lived in England, and that he was getting ready to leave for England on Friday week. Molly had told him that everything was in place for him to come to England, so I very quickly stopped dreaming and made the boldest decision that I had ever made and announced that I would be joining him. He had been led to believe, by Molly, that it would be OK to come over, and that he could stay with the grandparents of her new boyfriend, Tom Clarke. Despite this seeming like my dream was coming true, it was not an easy position for me to be in. Of course, whilst I'd been merely dreaming of going to England I would have thought that this was always going to be an easy decision to make and I would be rushing to get going but, now I'm having to bite the bullet, I found it a totally mind shattering thing to have to come to terms with. With everything whizzing around inside my head I knew that this time next week I would likely not be looking down at Dunganstown Castle or the lovely little church that nestled to the castle's west side. I would not look over the hills and would not be seeing Lugnaquilla and all of that beautiful scenery that stretched as far as the eye could see – the heather, the hawthorn and the ferns spreading over the hillsides. I suppose at the time I didn't appreciate it but from now on in I was going to have a different environment to deal with. I knew, from my trip to Manchester when I was 8 years old, that you wouldn't be able to have a conversation in the middle of the road as we did in Ireland in those days for example, so I knew things would be very different. I just didn't realise how different.

So, now I had to prepare and make my final arrangements. I went to say farewell to the people who were so much a part of my life as a young lad when I was working on Burke's Farm on Cullen Road, between Three Mile Water and Dunganstown near Wicklow. I went to say goodbye to Eva Heavener who owned the farm across the road from us and to Dick Cunningham, her farm helper. Of course, I had a lot of memories with the Heavener's. They kept their place and farmyard beautifully and the garden and the house itself were as if they were in a painting with all the lovely flowers in a huge range of colours. I remember particularly that they had two enormous Monkey Puzzle trees. Eva was the lady who would play the organ at the Three Mile Water church and if Mrs McDonald wasn't able to do Dunganstown church, then Eva would stand in and play the organ on the Sunday morning service. She was a lovely lady and my respect and fondness for her humanity lasted through all of my life until, sadly, she passed away a few years ago at a great age.

Next I went to see old Paddy Doyle and many people would have thought that it would take hell itself to throw him into the position where we said our long goodbyes but he seemed quite upset to see me go. This certainly wasn't the Paddy Doyle that I had known. I didn't know that he had a soft side at all as he would be the one that was always be shouting 'the curse of God on them' and so on. The funny thing is that I took my daughters to see him on holiday many, many years later and my eldest daughter, Debbie, can still hear Paddy's shrieking, dressing down a situation, as he would. She was only a child at the time but it still rings in her ears, as she was gob smacked by it all. We still have the craic about it at home.

Then it's on to Marie Doyle and her mother, Mrs Leonard, who kept the cats that used to bother Paddy because she used to feed them so well that none of the neighbours' cats would go too long without visiting Mrs Leonard. She had a lovely house and garden, with the path boards lined with the glass balls that used to be on the old fishing nets from the 17th century.

Of course, I couldn't go to England without going to see Maureen Slattery in the little shop at Three Mile Water. All the memories of her kindness (she couldn't say a bad word about anybody) came flowing back to me. I had the same surprising response as I'd had from the others. Where normally I would have had a nod and a quick word with her, this time I had the 'full Monty' with the kisses, the cuddles, the bear hugs and the hand shakes all wrapped up into one.

All this sentimental saying goodbye brought back lots of memories for me. I thought back to my time on Burke's farm, in Cullen Lane when I would not have had anybody annoying me except myself as I would have been working and living there mostly alone. But I had good food – and plenty of it! – for that period of my life. It was plain and wholesome. My diet there included plentiful supplies of the most beautiful potatoes you could imagine. If you've not tasted real Irish spuds, then you haven't lived. They're so floury and taste just great, eaten with absolutely anything. There was an Irish way of checking the quality of the spuds you were cooking – they had to 'laugh at you' by splitting as they cooked. Waxy spuds just wouldn't do, I'm afraid. I would also dig up carrots and cabbages then cook them myself for a great meal. Often I was also given, while I was on the farm, homemade jam – my favourite was one a neighbouring farmer's wife would make and that was Vegetable Marrow and Ginger Jam – scrumptious! Life would undoubtedly be very different where I was heading.

When I was saying goodbye to these people it was as if there was a different presence about. I can't really put it into words, but there was a deep, deep respect for me that I had had no idea existed. I'd planned a goodbye with the usual quick nod or a handshake but I found myself saying goodbye to these people with what could best be described as a bear hug – something that I had never experienced before. I felt very embarrassed and was totally at sea. Some even had tears coming down their faces. I could not get a handle on this at all because my background didn't involve bear hugs or warmth, love and respect – it was all foreign territory to me. I suppose they had seen many of the young lads leave and many of these young people were never to be seen again as it was only the odd one or two that ever returned to their lives in their Irish communities.

In preparation for having to find a new job in my new life, one evening I had a meeting with the vicar to obtain a last reference from him before destiny unknown takes shape. Prior to going to see the new vicar, Reverend Baird, I was known as Derek Donaldson – Donaldson being my foster parent's surname. To go in under that name and come out with a totally different name was certainly setting off into the unknown from a peculiar point. He told me what little he knew about my origins and this really shook me up. But I suppose there was something positive about this on that night. After seeing the Reverend Baird at least I could confirm that my mother existed, although he could not give me any help with whether I had a father, brothers and sisters, or uncles and aunts. All that would be something that would have to find its way into my life at a much later stage – but at least the new name and the few details he was able to give me were a start on my lifelong journey to find out just who I was. I had grown up not knowing anything about my background so I accepted this lack of information as a negative alongside the positive of the bit that he was able to give me.

After coming through the dark tunnels of my upbringing that I had managed to survive I could easily consider myself lucky to be at the juncture where I was then. Now a whole new world was about to open up for me, so I set out to confront my destiny.

Chapter 1

Destiny tapping on my shoulder

My big adventure was about to begin, my dreams would now start to come true as I made my escape from the hell of my childhood. So, with only a half-baked idea of what to expect, my foster father and I headed for England to meet up with my foster sister, Molly, in Market Harborough. We were catching a boat from Dunlaoghaire to Holyhead, and my mind was in overdrive, sieving and sorting as to whether or not I was doing the right thing. Worrying as I always did. You see, no matter how bad things are for you where you are, (for example, working at the Burke's farm, on Cullen Road at least whilst I was there I had a bed, a roof over my head, and food to eat) none of these things were guaranteed. Although I worried to myself then, it is only when you look back at your life from a more comfortable vantage point nearly 50 years later that you realise how close you came to falling into boundless bouts of hopelessness, and sheer-face falls of glacial rock many thousands of feet below. You just don't know that you are skating by, escaping disaster and devastation by a fluke that's the thickness of a hair. When you're older and have come through the trickier parts of life, you can only thank God and think how lucky you have been in that world that covers destinies unknown. There is no doubt I have been extremely lucky in that I have managed to survive the pulling powers of total destruction, as there were so many laid in my path. As I did not have the education, the ability to communicate or an awareness of how to intermingle with my fellow human beings, the simple fact of my survival goes to show how very, very lucky I have been.

But, of course, it would be wrong to assume that I personally was the only one that could have encountered these unknown destinies. That is not the case. All people, irrespective of what their education is or is not, would have to deal with that same old foe – destiny unknown. There are no road signs to guide you through life, or maps to assist you, so you simply have to be a victim of your own life's perils.

Anyway, armed only with the lack of all of this knowledge, we caught the train at Wicklow Station and headed for Dunlaoghaire. Funnily enough, this was only the third time I had been on a train in my life, but the trip whizzed by and so this was an excitement – and a worry – in itself. Then, before I knew it, we had to get ready to transfer to the mail boat from Dunlaoghaire to Holyhead.

Isn't it odd, too, that just over 10 years earlier we had been getting the cattle boat to Birkenhead on our way to Manchester in 1949? The differences from our journey on that occasion that I can vaguely remember were quite massive but one little thing in particular sticks in my mind about the boat to Birkenhead. I had been just a young lad at the time and my memory of the cattle boat was of the funny little holes in the tables for mugs to sit in to save them from falling off, but that feature was absent from the mail boat those few years later. But, as they say, time and tide wait for no man. I do not really remember a large amount about being on the boat in February 1960. I suppose I was too deeply immersed in my thoughts as to what our destiny was going to be, and probably the cold light of day had dawned on me and made me concentrate on whether this venture was indeed a good idea or not.

Next, we got on the mail train to Rugby and this had a different effect on me. My mind was thrown back through the years. As we whipped along the tracks through the villages, towns and cities, my thoughts went back to when we were in Manchester and I had seen all of the bombsites from the war years all around. I wondered what it would have been like then to be on this same train during the war with no lights in the towns as you passed through, or being on the train itself in fear of being a bombing target. I suppose these are silly things to be thinking of but nevertheless, they leave a mark on you as a young person and you don't forget what life was like for people in the UK during those war years. With all the noise of the train swishing along, packed to the gunnels, you were not just thinking of your own destiny, you also cast a thought as to what the destinies were going to be for your fellow passengers. Where were they going? Why were they going and what awaited them? My imagination was working overtime – as always. For me this train journey was awesome – coming down on the train and being able to see those vast areas of towns and cities that were lit up as if an enormous light was hanging from the sky. My mind wandered back to my childhood, seeing the lights of a little old car or tractor making its way along an Irish lane and disappearing out of sight. But now, sitting on the train, it was as if a large screen at a picture house was relaying all those images and lights for me to wonder at. How they jumped and popped about, and I wondered how could this huge lighted area be possible, after me coming from a lonely little lane with a few lights in the distance. Back in Ireland, in comparison, the lone light would be like somebody was having a smoke in a bush. I suppose these are the kinds of things that can wander through your mind as you make your way to a new life.

Eventually, there we were, the train squeaked and crackled and came to a halt in Rugby Station, where, of course, Molly and her new boyfriend, Tom Clarke, had arranged to meet us. I have to say that when my foster father set eyes on Molly's boyfriend he was not overjoyed or impressed by his likely son-in-law to be. In fairness to my foster father it would not have been difficult to work out that this relationship was not going to be a bed of roses. Poor old Tom Clarke had that unfortunate ability to make it obvious that it was not a good experience that was in store for us. He was so full of his own importance that, if he'd been right, he should have been able to give you a piggyback ride to the moon but obviously he wouldn't even be able to get airborne. I am sure that the meeting with Molly and her boyfriend was not an inspiring start to our new life in England for my foster father but putting all that on one side, we still had to make our way, in their company, and as their guests, to Market Harborough, so on we went.

Tom Clarke had borrowed his grandparents' lovely Hillman Minx motorcar for the journey to Market Harborough. When some people borrow someone else's motorcar they seem to want to drive it in a manner that is not fit for banger racing and they have no regard to wrecking someone else's pride and joy. Lo and behold, Clarke was this type of person; he had that awful lack of consideration of the fact that his grandfather would have spent his life earning the money that would make it possible for him to have that car to take his wife out on a Sunday afternoon drive. You would have thought, if anything, that whoever borrowed it would have driven it with extra care but we were soon to find out that such care did not exist as Molly said to him 'why don't you show them how we drive over here?' And he was more than happy to comply.

Hurtling through South Kilworth, North Kilworth and Thedingworth, we seemed to be sliding through the corners at breakneck speed and being guests of theirs, we did not wish to appear to be 'back seat drivers' so we kept quiet, clung on and just hoped that they would steady up a bit so that we might all land in one piece. However, things got worse and between Thedingworth and Lubenham, on the way to Market Harborough, disaster struck and we suddenly found ourselves tumbling about in the car. The car flipped over onto its side three times and we all had to climb out through the door that was now facing up to the sky. I was horrified to see that we had narrowly missed a telegraph pole. We were all extremely badly shaken up, shocked, battered and bruised, and my foster father stood, visibly shaken, his hand resting in the doorjamb to straighten himself up and gather his senses. Clarke was the last one to climb out of the car and as he did so he pulled the door down, thus trapping the older man's hand in the jamb. This must have been excruciating and it left my foster father with four very black, broken fingers.

As we stood there, dazed, wondering what to do, a chap that Clarke had overtaken just before the crash stopped his car and offered some rum to see if it would restore life back into us and he commented 'My God, what were you doing, why were you driving like that when the roads are like sheets of ice?'

We then gratefully took up his offer to take us to the Cottage Hospital on the Coventry Road in Market Harborough and we slithered across the road to his car as the ice was making it so slippery. Of course, when you consider destinies, we had not taken any of these happenings into account and his injury meant that my foster father was going to be unable to work for many months, which put a further spanner in the works. I know I thought at the time 'surely things cannot get any worse'. But, lo and behold, we were to discover that they could.

We found that we were, in fact, unexpected – and unwanted – guests at the home of Molly's boyfriend's grandparents and that Molly had made no arrangements at all for us to stay with them, especially me. There was a great deal of bad feeling in the air, which you could taste as well as hear – it was the sort of climate that I truly dreaded and I had great difficulty in coping with; a situation where I knew I was not wanted. I suppose this could be traced back to my earlier life and the experiences I was forced to endure.

However, things went a touch in my favour when Clarke's granny – who, incidentally, worked at Simon's, the world-famous corset factory that is now the library and council offices in Market Harborough – accepted that I would be able to stop on condition that I would pay for my digs. I suppose, when you think about it, the poor woman could have assumed that not only was she having to keep her grandson and his girlfriend but now had her father and an unwanted foster brother into the bargain, and when you consider all of that, it would not have been unreasonable for her to be very concerned that she was being dumped on.

But, of course, saying you will be paying for digs is one thing and, of course, I genuinely wanted to pay my way, but it is another to be able to do that on an ongoing basis. I had £10 to my name when I set out to catch the train, then the mail boat, and the mail train to Rugby. Although it would not have been a huge fare to pay out of a tenner, it most certainly would have made a substantial hole in it, and remember that this money would have to last me until I got work, so that made me worry even more. I felt sick with worry.

So, what an introduction to my new life. I had arrived in the place of my dreams only to find that it not only contained the family and financial problems that I had always been plagued by, but also that it was a vastly different place to what I was used to. The traffic was horrendous and everything just seemed so strange. And now, with my extra problems and feeling so unwelcome and out of place, I would have to find a job in double-quick time.

Chapter 2

First things first

My first priority had to be getting a job to support myself and my foster father – especially now that he wasn't in a position to support himself and also as we hadn't brought much in the way of money with us. Things were getting desperate. Of course, getting work for an uneducated, ignorant ex-slave from Ireland was not going to be an easy task, and destiny could begin to unfold. What I did not realise was that, at the time, if you were 18 years of age you were on call-up for National Service. Being an Irish subject would have made no difference to me being called up as it would not have exempted me, and of course, employers were aware of the rules governing call-up. Ireland had signed a Treaty with the UK that all Irish citizens would be treated as equal citizens in the UK whilst they resided there and after six months the British Government could call them up for National Service.

Even today, a lot of people are not aware of this being the case, and oddly enough many men from Ireland were in the Second World War through that Treaty, as well as the Korean War and all the other wars that followed it.

So, in my forthcoming job search, which was becoming more urgent by the minute, I had the possibility of National Service against me; I also had my lack of education working against me because wherever I went I was usually required to fill in an application form for the job. This came as a shock to me and made job-hunting a nightmare. Whenever they came to me with an application form to fill in I would be gone like a shot as I would have been too embarrassed and too full of shame to have to ask for their assistance in filling this form in. But I couldn't let any of this stop me, so I started the search straight away.

I had heard of a job at Market Harborough Council as a road sweeper. When I went to see the boss of the department he said he had indeed got a job for a road sweeper, but he did not have any intention of giving such a job to me as I should go and get myself qualified for a better one. But, of course, he could not have known what an impossible task, at that time, that would have been for me. He also couldn't begin to appreciate that for me to have landed that job as a road sweeper would have been like winning the lottery twice over after the conditions I had been used to all my life. My daily life had included pulling my feet out of clay pitted fields, bog-like ploughing, and fetching cows in when you would sink to your waist in some of the gateways. Working as a road sweeper on hard surfaces would have been heaven in comparison, but that person did not give me the job for what he thought was the best of reasons. He simply thought I could do better. It just shows that none of us always has the right answer when dealing with some of these complex matters.

When a person is telling you that a job is not right for you it may be very sensible advice, and when he is saying it to someone in a strange country who was desperately in need of a job of any sort, then, as they say, beggars can't be choosers. In my case this was destiny unfolding in all its anger, with all its force, sometimes positively and many more times negatively. But it is odd, no matter how dark the tunnel you are looking down, when it comes to surviving you just pull yourself up and head for the next obstacle. I never let up because it's in my make-up I would always be trying to make myself secure, looking for a safety net, just in case something went wrong. I guess it is a result of my upbringing. The uncertainties that I had to endure in my childhood left me very cautious, and my mind very raw, and so I was very aware of the need for simple survival.

After going down lots more blind job-search alleys, I next went down to Springer's Engineers in Market Harborough, makers of ornamental gates and storage tanks, where I wasn't confronted with application forms, or anyone deciding as to whether I should have a better job or not. Anyway, after going through all of the doors that were closed and all of the hopelessness of my case, I ended up making parts for ornamental metal garden gates on a jig. I would then have to have those parts spot welded by an experienced welder and then dip the gates into the paint tank of the colour that was required. Of course, finding yourself in this situation where your feet were on concrete and you weren't up to your neck in cow dung and fields of mud, was a bit of a bonus for me. Probably the most important of the differences (and believe me there were many) was to be paid regularly at the end of the week for the hours that you had worked. This was quite revolutionary to me, and even more unbelievable was that if you worked overtime you got paid for that too. But don't run away with any illusions that this job was like an office job where you could go to work in your best suit and tie – that you most certainly could not do. Because of dipping the gates and handling the wet paint afterwards, you could end up in a most sticky working position and you could not go and wash it off with soap and water. The wretched stuff stuck to you like glue.

When he gave me the job, the foreman had told me that he would have me trained up to do the spot welding and the welding on the storage tanks. But, unfortunately as always, I would have that old shadow, destiny, following me, which had a habit of turning everything upside down. In this case, the foreman's cousin turned up from Scotland and yes, you have guessed it; Derek was not going to be taught how to do welding on this occasion. I missed out again.

Being paid every week was a huge step forward, and enormous progress for me, but again the flip of the dice can change things you had not even thought about and problems were just around the corner. With the crash at Lubenham, which put my foster father out of work for months with his smashed hand, and with my foster brother back in Ireland driving the old aunts, Daisy and May, to despair (he was repeatedly not attending school at the Christian Brothers in Wicklow, and seemed to be well on the way to learning another 'trade' – how to rob and con people), I felt under pressure to sort things out, especially as the aunts had been very good to me when I was a child and I knew the problems Sean would be causing them. I thought of Daisy with her lank, black hair, stating loudly just what she thought of the situation and May, quietly working to try to put Daisy's wishes into action. They were what you might call 'characters', who I would credit with a large contribution to my survival as a child and for sure they did not deserve the trouble Sean would be bringing to their doorstep. I also knew the stress that this whole situation was causing my foster father and it left me no option but to seek an even better paid job than the one I was currently in. I knew I had to try again – and even harder. Because of all the problems he was causing back in Wicklow, the plan now would be to try and save enough money to get Sean over to England so that we could keep an eye on him and find him a job. Our aim was to check his runaway streak, and see if we could dampen it down.

I suppose a lot of people would wonder why I would be bothered about my foster father, whether he was stressed or not, knowing what had happened as I grew up as a child in Ireland, but you must never underestimate growing up in a family, even though it isn't your own – you are submerged into that family with normal honour and loyalty. In my case I must have had more than my fair share of honour and loyalty, of course, but he was the only father I had ever known and no matter what he had done to me I had such a deep down feeling of loyalty that I would have defied death to protect him. I know that sounds mad but, in all honesty, I grew to love my foster father and could not have loved my real father any better. So, yes, destiny does show up in very odd colours and certainly is totally unpredictable.

Although I was new to the Market Harborough area, I quickly settled down and knew I had to get myself out and about to make a life for myself. I checked out the boxing situation in the area very early on and soon started training with the Market Harborough Amateur Boxing Club. This was so important to me and put me in touch with the local boxing scene as well as helping to keep me fit. In an attempt to broaden my horizons I also, some would say surprisingly, joined the local Territorial Army unit. Although this might seem an unlikely choice for a lad from Ireland who had great difficulty following rules, keeping to time and so on, it had a great impact on my life. I believe that the TA influenced me in many ways. It made me be controlled – for the first time in my life – and it certainly made me less difficult to deal with and less rebellious. In the TA I found that I had to conform to their rules and I even, for the first time in my life, cleaned my boots! Joining the TA was one of the best things I have done in life.

Although I had settled down well enough, life in Market Harborough in those first few months was not without its difficulties, of course. One of the problems I had to cope with in those early days involved my health. Generally I was strong and healthy but I had the occasional tricky spell and, of course, the odd accident to contend with. One such difficult time occurred when I was in Cromer with the Territorial Army. The first night I arrived in camp I was taken extremely ill during the night and when they fetched the army doctor he suggested I should go into Cromer Cottage Hospital and have my appendix removed. Of course, this sort of thing you don't plan and do not even give a thought for, but how quickly disaster and danger can come and tap you on the shoulder. But I must say here and now that whilst I was in Cromer Cottage Hospital they looked after me as if I were a king. There was nothing that was too much trouble for them to do, and they were all very jolly and friendly people. Before having the operation, I insisted on seeing a Church of Ireland vicar. I cannot explain what was going through my mind at this point except to say that I have always been the sort of person that liked a safety net laid out in case anything went wrong, and having my appendix removed was as serious as it gets as far as I was concerned, so I desperately needed to have a Church of Ireland vicar come and see me. As I lived in what I believed to be a Protestant country I thought this would no trouble whatsoever but, in actual fact, they had no idea what I was talking about. They had never heard of a Church of Ireland vicar and there was not going to be time to get one over on a boat from Ireland. I was very worried and disgruntled with this situation but things were about to get worse. I was informed that on this particular occasion even the Church of England vicar was not available so they arranged for a Presbyterian vicar to come and see me. I might tell you I was not amused and thought things had come to a very low pitch in life for me to have to make such a sacrifice.

There was even more bad news to come my way. As I was waiting for the operation they came to me and said that I had to be shaved in a very private place. Now, when you are raised as I had been this would not have been a very funny predicament to be in. Two men turned up with their shaving bowls and razors and at this point I almost wanted the vicar who came in to pray for me whilst I was having the operation to reverse all that and let me die now. But I suppose, like everything, you have to shut your eyes and grin and bear it and pray to God that nothing like this should ever happen to you again.

After all that drama, to my surprise, after the operation when I woke up I was still on this planet. All the time I was in hospital I didn't have any visitors (apart from, eventually, some TA girls – but more of that later) even though I spent my birthday in there and there wasn't so much as a card or note from any of my family. That didn't come as any surprise to me – I wasn't missing anything as I had never got birthday cards anyway! But it wasn't all misery. I had the misfortune, if you could call it that, for my bed to be next to a Cockney chap and, of course, I had never heard a Cockney accent except on the radio before (but I suppose he would think that the Irishman spoke with a funny accent too, thinking about it). But once that poor Cockney spoke, that was me done for. I could not stop laughing. I would howl with laughter and the nurses would plead with the Londoner to speak quietly so I couldn't hear him for fear of me bursting my stitches. The laughing didn't burst my stitches but it did cause me to get an infection in my wound, which meant I had to stop in the hospital for two extra weeks. Life is never straightforward and at this point my life was certainly racing along. At the time, these things – such as the relatively short spell I was working at Springer's Engineers or the time I was at Market Harborough Boxing Club – seemed to last forever but, looking back now, I can see that my life went through a lot of changes in a very short space of time. When I recovered I had to get straight back to work, after a very short period of convalescence, at Parker's Grass Drying Plant where I had recently found a job.

All three of us – me, my foster father and Clarke – had found jobs at the Parker's Stamford Grass Drying Plant near Welford just before I had gone into hospital. This was part of my never-ending quest to get myself a better job with more money. Here at Parker's we were able to start together, doing seasonal work at the grass drying plant. This was a great opportunity for my foster father, Tom Clarke and me to get the start and, of course, in this job I was more than doubling my wages, as they worked 12-hour shifts – 12 hours on days and 12 hours on nights. My foster father and Tom Clarke took the inside jobs in the mill where they used to dry the grass and then pulp it into dust for mixing into cattle food. I got the job carting the newly mown grass to the dryers.

At this point then, with me back at work at the Grass Drying Plant after my operation, things were looking up. My foster father's hand was better and he was able to earn money and, equally, Clarke was able to earn better money than he had done before, as he did not usually like 'staying the course'. However, despite the plans that you may make in your mind there is always something that is working at a faster speed than you could imagine that throws all your plans upside down. Yes, I suppose it's that word destiny again, and it goes all the way through your life like a big black cloud ready to drop on you whenever it decides to do so. It has total control and you just have to go along with it and be a victim as and when. What dropped on us this time was a most surprising decision made by Molly –

she had decided that now she was going to get married. Her timing was impeccable, as this was just when her father had managed to get a few pounds together, and her husband-to-be likewise. Also, by now Sean was over from Ireland, although he couldn't help with the family budget at this point, as he was not allowed to work, being under fifteen years of age. Molly could change her mind like the wind so I was a bit suspicious about this decision at this time. Never one to follow a planned route, Molly, prior to meeting Clarke, had been going out with a sailor, who was supposed to be 'the one', but that all came to an abrupt end for some reason unknown to me. But now she insisted that marriage to Tom was what she wanted – and what she wanted, she got.

Molly was living in the school where she was working in Market Harborough, but she was not very keen on being governed by their rules, so I suppose when she had a chance to go with Tom Clarke to live in his grandparent's old detached town house on the Leicester Road, near the pond field, it meant that by doing so she would not have to worry about the school regulations in terms of what time she had to be in and so on. So you see that destiny, in its way, showed Molly the route that was convenient to avoid the other restrictions in her life in order to have a roof over her head at all costs.

Of course, Molly was entitled to live her life as she chose but it is one thing people having their own mayhem to live with, but it's another to splash that in the paths of other people who then have to pick up the pieces. In this case it was me who was going to have years of bailing her out and seeing where I could help her pay her gas, electric and rent bills. As regular as clockwork she would make a beeline for me to get help regarding these problems. At this point I was now having to work even longer hours than the 12 hours shifts in order to get money to cope with all of these family problems that I was having to resolve, even though, in reality, there is no blood connection whatsoever between me and my foster family. I did all these things but I was to find out, many years later, that they had no respect for me. I was merely a convenience for resolving their problems.

In any event, wedding expenditure at this point in time was certainly not my main priority. I was trying to save money for me to be able to buy my own vehicle because I always feared that Clarke, who gave me a lift to work, would get tired and pack the job in, like he had done with all his other jobs, which would mean that I would be left high and dry for a lift. As we had to travel 20 odd miles to the job that was not an easy thing to resolve as there was no bus or train service to that particular place.

But, as I said earlier, I had a great deal of commitments helping my foster family, and life was never short of surprises. I had noticed for some weeks that it did not matter how much money I earned, or had managed to save from the previous weeks, that the money in my wallet never got any greater. Of course, as I was not accustomed to having bank accounts or post office accounts, I had not got around to paying proper attention to what was going on, but when I did I got the shock of my life.

I had helped to get my foster brother over from Ireland, but what I did not expect to happen, after being on nights, was to be woken in the daytime to find Molly and Sean relieving my pay packet of some of the money I had saved! For those of you who have read my first book, 'Hannah's Shame', you would think there have not been any great changes or surprises there, but I can't to this day get my head around that situation. I would always want to see the best in everybody and did not want to have to accept that my foster brother and foster sister were robbing me so blatantly and deliberately. I had difficulty in becoming fully awake at that point and then in understanding, in my confused, sleepy state that this was being done to me by the people I believed would die for me, as I would have done for them. I cannot describe how shocked and frustrated I was in finding that this was going on. I think I have always had a problem in accepting the realities of life and even now I don't know why I didn't hate them, or want to punish them, for stealing from me. But, as you will find out later, I kept trying to help them and change them. I just knew, after this discovery, that I would have to take more care of my money.

Although I had not been living at 17 Leicester Road, Market Harborough very long, things were moving at a tremendous speed. The mother of a friend of mine, Johnny

Parker, a very able boxer, who worked at the Grass Drying Plant and lived in Clay Coton, Northamptonshire, offered to put my foster father up at her house. The reason for this being such a relief to me was that the signs were starting to show that Clarke was getting tired of getting up and being at work, after driving over 20 miles, for six o'clock in the morning. As he had never done anything like that in his life before, it just became too hard a task for him and very soon after this he packed in working at the Grass Drying Plant. Had my foster father not had the digs in Clay Coton, he would also have had to leave his job, as he would have had no transport. It was great for him to have this chance to stay in work but, of course, that left me in a fix because I was still living with Clarke's grandparents and had no transport for myself. A problem I had to solve – and quickly.

I was telling this to one of the people I met, a man called Edgar who lived in Sibbertoft. He was a very keen motorcyclist who had a number of bikes, one of which was a 1957 Mayflower Douglas, the chrome on which was polished to such an extent that you could have shaved as you looked into it. It was one of the most beautiful bikes I have ever seen, with horizontal pots very similar to the BMW. Edgar also had a 1939 BSA 250 ex-military bike, which he said he would sell to me in order that I would have transport and not have to rely on other people taking me about. I could become independent. Although my ignorance may sound amazing I had no idea that a 1939 ex-military motorbike may not have been the most reliable piece of kit to get me to work. But isn't youth bliss? None of this ever crossed my mind. Edgar brought the bike to the Grass Drying Plant and I paid him the few quid he wanted, but in all honesty, even if the bike had been standing against a new bike it would never have crossed my mind that it was 21 years old. I never had any idea that you had to adjust chains or change oil; the only thing I ever bothered about was filling it with petrol, which, in those days, was probably less than 4/6d a gallon.

Where I lived in Leicester Road there was a flight of steps from the road up to the house and no place near to the house where I could park the bike, so I asked the landlord at the Six Packs, the local pub, about one hundred yards along the A6 towards

Leicester, if I could park there and he gave me permission to park in one of his sheds. Setting off from the pub in the mornings, I would freewheel down the slope from the Six Packs onto the Leicester Road before trying to start the bike in order that I never caused any grief to anyone with the engine noise – at 5.45 am it would not have been the nicest noise to hear and would not have made me the most popular lad in Market Harborough!

I rode that bike for many months backwards and forwards and it never gave me a spot of trouble, but then it started to play up in a spectacular fashion. I did not often see Edgar as he was on a different shift to me. However, this particular day I met him as I was starting days and he was finishing nights. He asked me how the bike was going and I told him it was going great. He asked to see how it was and I started it up, but no sooner had I got it going than it backfired and went up in flames. The position I was in, with the bike not on its stand, meant that I could not let go of it so I grabbed Edgar's cap, which had that much grease on it you could have scraped it off with a knife, and was trying to put the flames out with that.

Luckily there was another lad on the shift standing close by, Dave Cheney, who lived at Swinford, and he had the good idea of getting handfuls of wet grass that had been got in from the previous shift, and covering the bike with them. Without this action most certainly both the bike and myself would have been severely burned, probably fatally, because there was no way that I was going to let that bike go until the flames had stopped coming out of it and, of course, there was a good chance that the building we were standing by would also have gone up in flames. Anyway, fate was on my side that day. Dave and I were not really the best of friends as he found it difficult to cope with my rawness, but I have to say I was eternally grateful for his help on that particular day. Edgar was a very keen motorcyclist and knew what he was doing in terms of restoring them. He soon sorted out the bits of burnt wire and replaced them and I was off again as if nothing had ever happened.

Soon after this shock, one night coming home from work, the old bike finally gave up the ghost. I had started climbing the hill between Lubenham and Market Harborough when the bike just blew up, never to go again. I'd had enough so I went off to the motorbike shop on the Kettering Road, which was owned by an ex TT rider, where I purchased a 1953 BSA250. God, did I think I was swanking it on this beast of a machine! I even got so confident that I wanted to take my test, so I arranged for this to take place in Kettering. With all of the rest of my life running around me, and coping with keeping all the balls in the air, I was now going to take a test to get a motorbike licence. For somebody like me this was like taking a trip to the moon and back. Who could have expected an idiot like me to get this far?

So, the test was arranged and I turned up in Kettering town at the examiner's office. He said that I had to do a figure of eight and the next time he saw me he would jump out in front of me and I had to apply my brakes and do an emergency stop. Of course, I had no idea what this figure of eight business was and just took the directions of the guy waving his arms in the direction I was assuming he would want me to take. I thought to myself that this fellow either has to be very brave or a complete idiot, because my brakes were not the best and for anyone to jump out in front of me without giving some notice, well, there was a very good chance of me taking him for a spin with the front wheel of the bike between his legs and him sitting on the mudguard as we went through Kettering town!

However, on this day I was spared that experience because I set off to do my 'figure of eight' and by the time I got back in the afternoon he said it was too late to do any more of the test and that I would have to come back and take another one. To say the least, I was not amused but, of course, with my background I would have difficulty in trying to understand his stubbornness in wanting me to take another test. After all, I had been out for ages trying to find this 'figure of eight' before I could find my way back and I thought if he had a heart at all he would just have given me the blessed licence, but he was not having any of it.

The next time I took the test I had found out more about the figure of eight business and had done a few trial runs at it before the day of the test dawned. I took the test and passed it, and my God I was so elated. I suppose if I had been more switched on, and had not got used to being over confident, I would have been better equipped and prepared for the first test. It is all too easy to become too confident and there are times when it pays to be more cautious.

Another accident was to befall my foster father. Unfortunately, he had some bags of grass meal fall on him from a very great height at work. Those bags were stacked to the gunnels, which would be 25 to 30 feet high, and they burst. This grass was crushed down to dust, so when a bag burst there would be a green fog everywhere. He became ill as a result of this. There was some gossip that there were people messing around and that is what caused the accident to happen. However, the result was that he ended up getting tuberculosis, but whether that was directly to do with the accident and the dust, or whether it was to do with his wife dying from TB and the infection lying dormant within him until the accident, we will never know. He was taken to Hatton Sanatorium near Warwick and, obviously, this brought back horrible memories for me (and for my foster father, of course) of my foster mother dying of TB. He finally recovered from this dreadful disease, as obviously they had made great medical strides in curing the disease in the years since she had died in 1952.

In the months that he was off work ill, I had to help pay for my foster father's digs in Clay Coton, so that was back to the norm of the responsibilities that were given to me as part of the family. Unfortunately he was missing his aunts, Daisy and May, so much, and the fact that he couldn't work as he was convalescing, meant that he was pining to get back to Dunganstown and County Wicklow. Daisy and May had spoiled him rotten when he was a child and, of course, their mother would have done likewise. No matter, going back to his aunts and the old hometown was what he longed for. I remember my foster brother and foster sister saying at the time how important it was to get him home and I agreed with this. At this time they were both working, as I was, but neither of them was prepared to offer a penny towards his fare home, even though they were his blood son and daughter, whereas I was the unwanted foster child who was considered the poor idiot. But that poor idiot was left with the decision to pay for his fare or not to do so. It was simply a duty I felt that I had to do, and I would not have given a second thought to having to meet that responsibility irrespective as to whether I was his blood son or not. So, with my foster father incapable of looking after himself I had, once again, to dig deep and use the money that I was saving to either buy myself a car or for a deposit for a house. I always felt very insecure in digs and I longed to be able to buy my own place – that was my number one priority. But once again I would have to sacrifice my own desires in order to carry out what I believed to be my duty and responsibility, as his foster son, to give him help when he needed it.

Shortly after my foster father went back to Ireland, I moved out of Leicester Road and went to live in Clay Coton, Northamptonshire. By now Molly was married to Clarke and Sean was working in the stores at a garage so things seemed to be looking up, but for me, of course, life never did seem to get better for very long. Clarke had left the Grass Drying Plant at this point and had managed to get a job at the railway shunting yard in Market Harborough. As you might have guessed by now, Molly wouldn't settle for staying with his grandparents for a minute longer than necessary, so she made him get a house with the railway in Rutland. This seemed like a major step forward for Molly and her family but as Clarke was in some ways very similar to my foster father, he got tired of work very quickly so things were never going to run smoothly. Of course, with a child now on the scene for Molly and Clarke, when they came to me for money to pay their rent, electric and gas arrears, it only made it more difficult for me to say no. I remember going to visit them one very cold, icy, snowy Easter and there was not a spark of fire and no firewood to be seen in the place. They were all frozen, including the child. As Clarke was working at the railway yard at this point, I would have thought that he could have found a solution to this problem himself – but no. You see, at this time in Britain they were a lot later converting to diesel trains than in Southern Ireland so coal was available to him. I suppose the late conversion would have been to do with the coal mining industry and the availability of coal, so in the early 60s there were still plenty of steam trains running up and down the country and, of course, like all government run organisations they had no concern for economy or preventing waste, so with all these trains passing through the level crossing in Bourne village there was as much coal as you cared to pick up flung all over the track, the finest coal you have ever seen. It would have been easy enough to pick up the coal in complete safety because Clarke controlled the level crossing. It just amazed me how they could be freezing to death and not do something constructive to sort out their own needs. But that was how they lived and it seemed to be my destiny to always have to make up for their shortcomings.

Chapter 3

Working for a Living

Work was always important to me and I continually strived to improve my lot in life. Of course, my commitment to my foster family also drove me to work in a variety of jobs in those early years in England with the need for money always pushing me on. In the summer that we were first over in England we, as I've said before needed work and so Clarke, my foster father and I headed for Parker's Grass Drying Plant near Welford. Of course, going into Parker's, a very spacious business and farm, I would immediately think back to those little boggy fields that I had left behind in Ireland, where every step you took you ended up adding inches to your height with the mud that would stick to your feet. This was a big advantage to me but apart from the lack of boggy fields, there were some other vast differences between working for them and the little farmers that I had worked for in Ireland. You were paid every week, but even though I worked a 12-hour shift, I still had to work overtime to make more money. As I was not yet 21 my pay was less than the 'adult' men who worked there. Nevertheless, I was earning nearly £20 per week – just 4p short of this princely sum – and I thought I was really rich having that sort of pay for a week's work. Of course, the natives and the ones over 21 would have had more money, but, unlike me, they would not think they were getting a lot. It just goes to show that fate has a funny deal and a lot depends on your point of view. The size of the set up impressed me too. Parker's Grass Drying Plant was an enormous affair to me after the little lanes and tiny, hedged fields in Ireland; I was now working in fields bigger than the whole farm I had worked on in my younger days. This was partly because of the clearing of all the hedges and ditches out of the farms. They seem to have started that process much earlier in England than in Ireland. In some of the fields there were over 100 acres and years ago there would have been a gated road through it with wooden fencing for miles. To my way of thinking it was the nearest thing to being a Texan Ranger! The size of the Parker's Grass Drying Plant and fields would certainly have been like a prairie in comparison to the little fields that I had known so well. The whole of Burke's farm was just over 70 acres and some of the fields at the Grass Drying Plant would have been over one hundred acres – it was a totally different environment.

Up on some of the high fields at the Grass Drying Plant you could see for miles. You could see Daventry and Rugby's radio masts as you were flying around the field on the night shift and your mind would run wild sometimes, wondering what the people would be doing in that part of the world as you chased after grass cutting machines. These machines were a make called New Holland and they would cut the grass and blow it into your trailer. This was assuming, of course, that you were alert enough to make sure you didn't miss the burst of grass that was being thrust into your trailer. Sometimes, if you dozed off a bit, or your mind was running in another direction and you weren't fully concentrating, you would hear the curses coming at you from your work mates for you to wake up. But after you had been working all night sometimes it was not as easy to be 'with it' as you might think and some nights were worse than others.

In my experience, when you move into a different society and environment you will always meet people who are very keen to have a good laugh at someone else's misfortune and in our case we were given unfortunate, but apt, nicknames while we were working at. You may remember that there used to be an advertisement for a breakfast cereal with elf-like characters called Snap, Crackle and Pop – well, my foster father was Pop, Clarke was Crackle and I was Snap. I suppose it may have been, in my case, not too wide of the mark as I was not very skilled at dealing with wisecracks and particularly if the fun side of it was at my expense! I suppose I would have been like a young crocodile snapping all the time when it would have been better if I had ignored it, but these are the sorts of things you have to learn along the way.

I suppose, in the early 60s, at Parker's Grass Drying Plant a normal day's work was a 12 hour shift and, in my case, there would be 20 odd miles to travel before I arrived and then back again after I had finished, so my working life was certainly not a bed of roses. As I say, the days were long, the journey to work was long, the nights were even longer, and yet I grew to love it. I learned to shape myself, or I was shaped into whatever situation I was confronted with, and I eventually learned to laugh and not take myself so seriously.

The farm manager, Mr Waters, who swanned around in his Land Rover, was considered at times to be quite cold in character, but I discovered that he had a bigger heart than he was given credit for. He must have told his wife that they had this half-starved Irish kid who was in desperate need of a good feed working with them. She arranged, after hearing my story I assume, to send cakes and wholesome sandwiches down to the farm for me. That was not something she had done for anyone else who worked on that estate – she didn't even do that for the Polish refugees, two of which used to live in one of the outhouses on the site. But something that touched her heart must have been said and I was very grateful for all I received. I was also very surprised, because I think this shows that, whatever my faults might have been, the people in charge considered me to be very loyal and enthusiastic about my work and my duty to others.

This loyalty and capacity for hard work showed itself in ways that showed that I was not like many of the others. They would be ready to go home an hour before finishing time. No matter what had happened I would never leave the field until I knew that the charge-hand and everyone else were on their way. In these circumstances I suppose some people might have thought that I was a creep, a boot licker, or whatever you want to call someone, but from my point of view it was just how work was. I was used to working 24/7 without even being paid for the ordinary hours never mind overtime. To me behaving like that in a work situation would be no more out of the ordinary than having a cup of tea. It is strange to think that at the time you are unaware that you are odd. What makes you odd is what the other people around you are used to. I was totally unaware that a charge-hand could be telling the plant manager anything good about me because I didn't grow up in the sort of environment where people praised you for anything. I simply would not have given any of it a thought. Similarly, isn't it strange that some of your mates would be thinking what a creep you were because you had done something that you would not have even thought about?

Working in the Grass Drying Plant were people from all over the villages and towns and, believe it or not, the farm manager reckoned that people from Rugby were no good. He had little time for them, as the ones he had had working for him in the past who came from Rugby used to wind him up something terrible because they were un-reliable. As I was living in Clay Coton I thought maybe it was good that I was not from Rugby! There were also Italians, Germans, Poles and Ukrainians and you just have to fit in. You have to learn quickly how everyone thinks. I found I could cope easily with the local-village-mentality thinking of the native English people, which, of course, in normal village life in Ireland would not really have been any different

After work cutting grass in the fields finished at the end of the season in October, we headed back to the farm for the spud picking. In the hovels the spuds were weighed and bagged, and it would be freezing cold. We would go onto the railway track that went through Stanford, near to Stanford Hall, and collect bags of coal, which we would then put into braziers made from punctured oil drums. That certainly brought a bit of warmth and happiness into our lives. We would pray for it to be wet when we were working nights because that would give you an easier night. If it was dead dry you would have to go like the clappers to keep the drying plant going and you would be coming round the corners into the drying plant yard to tip the grass on two wheels. This was a difficult skill to develop and not everybody was able to achieve it.

I remember my mate Smiggy having a very bad experience when it was a dry night and he was having to go like the clappers. The hydraulic pipe for elevating the trailer had burst, but instead of Smiggy turning the engine off, he had the engine running which meant that the pump was still pumping the hydraulic oil out at a hell of a rate. It looked as if he was coming through a hailstorm, he was that splattered with it. By the time someone could get to the tractor to turn it off poor Smiggy looked a sorry sight, plastered in hydraulic oil.

This was just one of the misfortunes that

would await you when you least expected. You would normally be able to hang your hat on the accuracy of everything being in place with the machines when you took over a tractor at the start of your shift, but sometimes you allowed yourself to get into that familiar comfort zone with disastrous results. One morning I got on the tractor to pull off, but the driver on the shift before me had left the trailer in front of the guttering on the shed, so when I pulled off the high piece of the trailer (there to stop grass blowing off the trailer) matched fair and square to the guttering. I heard this almighty crash, bang, wallop behind me. The noise was horrific. I thought a plane had crashed nearby and I could see all the people around me were running for their lives in all directions. What had happened was that the trailer had clipped the guttering as I pulled away and laid the lengths of guttering in a pile at the other end of the building. Being asbestos they made a terrific noise. Some people believed at the time that the other driver had deliberately left it in that position so the disaster would happen to whoever followed them in the driving seat. Of course, some of the workers were always up to some trick or other to brighten their working day. You would not even be able to imagine some of their tricks but they would take the Mickey out of you, and have a laugh at your expense. Sometimes they would even wee on your exhaust manifold so that when the engine got hot you would have a terrific stink wafting up your nose!

One of the biggest shocks I ever had was in the dead of night in a very bad fog in the middle of a one hundred acre field. The fog was so dense that trying to find the gateway to get back onto the road after filling up my trailer was a tough job. Sometimes you would not know where you were as, in addition to the fog problem, you would have been going round and round and the nearer you got to the centre of the field the more disorientated you got. On this particular night when I was struggling to find the gateway I caught in my lights a badger, but with the fog, the lights, and me being half asleep, it appeared to me to be like a monster. If I hadn't been firmly sitting down on the seat I would have fallen off the tractor with the shock. It wasn't until much later that I realised it had been just a harmless little badger.

In that job you could never win whether it was dead dry or soaking wet. You went like the clappers if it was dry but when it was wet the stuff would gather behind the wheels of the trailer. When you got on the road you would be leaving behind you the equivalent of a sleeping policeman in a mound of muck and grass. In those days, if you brought muck on to the road the farmer would have to make sure it was all cleaned up (not like today when there is no account-ability to anybody in this regard). And, of course, that was yet another job that would have to be sorted before you went home.

Even with a steady job like this, my life was not without its happenings and excitement. One Christmas time I bought a TV for the three cottages in Clay Coton because I had had a television in Market Harborough where I had stayed for a while. In those days there used to be the New Year Hogmanay Show with Jimmy Stewart and those great Scottish entertainers, the Alex Brothers, on their accordions. In these digs the other lodger was an old chap who was probably one of the most miserable and tightest people I had ever met. When he smoked a cigarette he would only ever smoke half of it and then stub it out and put the stub in his pocket. Most of the time we just tolerated each other but he would not have been happy with me when it was Hogmanay. The TV programme did not start until nearly midnight and I would be dying to see it but when he went to bed, just as it was starting, his grunts and groans certainly left me in no doubt that he would not be happy until I were forced to give up and go to bed myself. Now, fair enough, he was up early in the morning because he worked on the roads, but it was not as if I was making a noise or banging around because I just would not have done that. This would have been around 1962 and I wasn't in those digs for long but, my God, it seemed like years while I lived there.

Despite his displeasure, I stopped up for another half hour or so and watched the Hogmanay and then reluctantly went to bed. Of course, I did not stay up as long as I would have if it had been under different circumstances but I found that when I was in digs there were lots of occasions like this when I would long for my own place so I would not have to put up with other people's likes and dislikes.

In the early hours of that morning I woke up and saw flames coming up the stairs and, in my sleepy state, I thought it was Mrs Parker downstairs getting the fire going again, although I couldn't think why she would be doing that. Within a few seconds I realised that the flame-like flashes were a lot bigger and higher than you would expect from old Mrs Parker's little fire so I immediately jumped out of bed to see what was the matter. I soon smelled smoke coming in my direction and to my horror I realised there was a fire. I did the only thing I could think of at that moment and started shouting 'fire, fire, fire!' while charging down the stairs. To my horror, when I got to the bottom of the stairs I could see a fire raging in full flame. I decided to jump past the fire but in the end I took too big a jump for my own good, as I ended up past the doorway and into the scullery with a thunderous crash. With this little accident, plus the smoke and the flames, by the time I had found my way back to the door entrance I was in a state – stunned and a bit bruised and battered. But somebody else appeared at that point. That old grumpy chap that I always looked upon him to be, was as calm as a cucumber. He had got the door open and had started to take buckets of water from a large rain barrel and was dousing the fire. Of course, in those days very few people had a telephone so when young Mrs Parker – my landlord's daughter-in-law who lived next door – heard the commotion and got out of bed she ran to the telephone box in the village to call the fire brigade.

Whilst all this was going off Mrs Parker senior was upstairs and we were trying to persuade her to come out through the upstairs window so we could rescue her, but to our annoyance she would stick one leg out, then stick the other leg out to see if she could get onto the ledge so we could rescue her, taking up valuable time. In the end she shouted down at us that she was not going to jump out and break her neck, as she would prefer to die in the fire rather than going through that procedure. However, by the time she made that decision we had the fire out and she was able to come down the stairs. As she walked down the stairs it was difficult to see anything with clarity because of the smoke and all the panic and fuss going on downstairs. To add to the commotion two fire engines, complete with blaring sirens had now turned up to put out the fire that we had just about managed to put out ourselves. In the middle of this mayhem the younger Mrs Parker appeared through the smoke with my television in her arms. She was a very small woman and was carrying this huge TV I burst out, 'for goodness sake put it down - you will rupture yourself'. She told me she had to get my TV out as she knew I was paying for it weekly and that I would not want it going up in smoke!

What an honour to have known such brilliant people. But, as they say, when the going gets tough, the tough get going. They are the sort of people you like to look over your shoulder and see behind you, and to be fair to old Jack, as grumpy and mean as he was, he had perhaps saved my life with his calmness and single-minded focus with those buckets of water he fetched from the rain barrel. He went back and forward, calmly and with a determined look on his grumpy face, as if the whole thing was an everyday occurrence. I like to think also that I woke him up and perhaps saved his life too. So, I say, although you are now maybe in the next world Jack, I do remember you and also respect you because you may have saved my life. Good on you.

This was the nightmare that we all found ourselves in there in that quiet little village of Clay Coton in Northamptonshire. That night's 'entertainment' brought two fire engines from Rugby and caused plenty of upset in the village. The problem had been that Jack, being an economical smoker who only ever smoked half of a cigarette at a time and then put it out to make it last longer, hadn't fully extinguished the half cigarette, so it flared up later in the night and ignited the box of matches in his pocket. This meant that all the clothing on the coat stand became aflame, and to make matters worse the Christmas decorations were still up and they carried the fire across all angles of the room. I suppose we were very lucky that we ever got out of it alive.

Of course, in addition to being truly thankful and in awe of Jack's calm efforts, I have got to be extremely thankful to John's wife. She was the bravest of the brave with her care and consideration to me, knowing that had the TV gone up in the fire I would have been responsible for paying for it. I am afraid I have always been a telly addict to some degree since I first started watching it down in Cullen Lane with Paddy Doyle. Now that I had become accustomed to my own TV I would have been lost without it. Don't get me wrong, I did not have that much time to watch the television as I was going to work, playing skittles, going to the TA, and by now I was boxing again. All of these interests were pulling on my time, but to know that TV was there and that it was mine mattered a lot to me. Oddly enough, I would not have been too bothered if I had not seen even one programme in a week but being able to see it on the table was a nice feeling to me as I had grown up without the most basic of amenities. It was simply good to have it, just for me.

That fire was a big thing in my life at the time – as was Mrs Parker rescuing my TV – but there was always something going on and I never quite knew what was going to hit me next. But I was about to find out what destiny – in terms of a social life – had in store for me.

Chapter 4

An uneasy social life

As well as trying to improve my lot in life financially, I knew that I had to make an effort to build a social life for myself. However, my lack of social graces certainly made for an eventful time for me in my first few years in England. I went through life outside work in a state of continual anxiety. I worried what people thought of me, I was nervous about meeting new people – especially girls – and I was forever thinking that I was about to put my foot in it. And it wasn't just social graces I lacked – I didn't drink alcohol and in those days it seemed that this would have been the key to an easy social life. When two old ladies in Ireland, Mrs Freer and Miss McDonald, got me to sign a Teetotaller Pledge when I was ten years old, destiny could never have told me then how much more complicated that could make my life as a young man in England eight years later. But make things more complicated it did. I socialised with people of my own age but I went on my own and came back on my own, so I had no idea that, as far as my peers were concerned, I could have come from another planet. Mostly, it was my lack of experience in socialising with other people that caused this problem but my not drinking certainly made my life a great deal more difficult than was strictly necessary. It picked me out as an oddity but, of course, to me this wasn't odd so I couldn't understand most of what went on. But I suppose there was also another benefit to my not drinking that I didn't think of at the time. I think it kept me from getting into the wrong crowd, as they would say. But I was snubbed and sent into my little corner of isolation until I learned to grow above it all and to throw confusion into the path of those who would jeer at me for being an oddball because I never had to drink to be happy and enjoy myself. I have no doubt in my mind that I most certainly would not have been any happier if I had liked a drink.

But these are the sorts of problems that you encounter as you pass through this life, and nobody makes sure you are equipped to meet these sorts of challenges. For instance, a good education and the ability to integrate without being seen as an oddball, or a 'square' as it used to be in those days would have helped. However, I had my mate Smiggy who was around about my own age, but he came from a loving family and had had a normal up-bringing. He must have found me very difficult to get a handle on, as I don't suppose he had ever come across anybody like me who was so suppressed and so much outside normal society and civilisation. Looking back now I can see how difficult it must have been for him, but he never gave up wanting me to be more acceptable to the norm of the day and would take me to dances in the villages of Sibbertoft, Cold Ashby, Naseby and Wel-ford. I was always a huge, unexploded bomb as far as embarrassing him was concerned. Once he saw me saying goodnight to one of the girls that we had met at a dance one evening. He was appalled to see me kissing her with an open faced crash helmet and gloves on! Smiggy gave me a terrible dressing down for this and let me know that you did not do that sort of thing with the girls around there. He said I had to kiss them goodnight without the hat on and without the gloves. Of course, I could see no harm in any of it and could not understand the fuss. It was only afterwards that I realised, years and years later, what a goat I had been. But when you were so far out of the civilised loop these silly little things that would normally happen automatically would have to be rehearsed and it took many years after I arrived in England, because of what I had been through in Ireland, for my brain to catch up with where it should have been. It will be no surprise to know that, after that first disaster, Smiggy would always be looking in my direction with bated breath when it came time to be going and saying goodnight to the girls we had met at the various dances. (Oh, and just in case you wondered why we would be having crash hats and gloves on I suppose I ought to make it clear now that we both rode motorbikes at the time.)

Another thing that was very difficult was coping with landlords and landladies, as they would have their set routines and requirements and I had never had a set routine in my life prior to coming to England – never saw any need for them! They told me times for meals or times when the door would be locked and at first I took no notice. But I soon had to start to listen because they made me aware, in no uncertain terms, of the consequences of my ignoring their requests and rules. Oddly enough, as well as them pulling their hair out over my lack of compliance with routines, that same problem made me pull my hair out. I just could not see any reason for them to get excited just because I was not in at a time they thought I should be.

Of course this would cause quite a lot of problems, but in fairness to the landladies, well some of them at least, they occasionally showed signs of being able to understand my point of view. Most of them liked the few bob coming in from having lodgers and would often long for their own independence so they had sympathy with me at times. On the other hand, many of them had not looked after young people for many a long day – and certainly not one like me! Then they found it quite difficult and annoying to have to cope with someone who looked on life in an entirely different way. These landladies would all vent their frustration with me without me ever having the slightest idea why they were upset. The first I would know about having caused an upset was when there would be a bang and a wallop down in the kitchen, which I knew was extra to what was necessary and was just done to get my attention. So, the dark clouds of being unwanted would again be descending around me and then I would have to find a way of making them laugh and forget about the nuisance they thought I was.

There would be many times when I was in digs when you could cut the atmosphere with a knife. I knew deep down that I wasn't wanted but I found that when it came to me actually leaving the lodgings they would not want me to leave. I found this really confusing and it was, to me, very disturbing. I would still get on with my everyday life but mostly, whilst I was in digs, there was a very uneasy peace. I never really felt secure. I never felt wanted other than for a short while but whether this was down to my feeling insecure in myself or because of my actual experiences, I don't know. Because I was young and in digs in England I always felt the same and I was always trying to save a few bob so that I could buy my own place. That was a burning ambition of mine and it would be one of the reasons that made me so distressed and frustrated with my foster family. They were such a drain on me right from the time when I first arrived in England. So, trying to achieve my goal of getting a deposit for a house of my own one day always seemed to go further and further away from me. I was also always trying to save for transport, a car or something maybe one day. Owning my own home and transport were my driving ambitions, but as I was uneducated I knew I had to take jobs that did not pay a great deal so I had to work many hours overtime to make a difference to my situation – and sometimes just to make a living at all, with no luxuries or extras like transport at all.

Incidentally, my main diet while I was in digs over the years, was bread and jam, jam being, as they say, a poor man's ham! This was in sharp contrast to the plentiful and varied food I had enjoyed while working on the farms as a young teenager immediately before I came to England. If you've read my first book you might have expected me to be impressed with the food in England as I had been poorly looked after in this regard as a child but food on working Irish farms at that time was lush, tasted great and there was no shortage of it! After that, bread and jam seemed a real step down. However, life at this time wasn't all poor food, drudgery and disappointments. One weekend Smiggy suggested that we should head to Nottingham Goose Fair – the biggest fair in the UK. There were miles and miles of it – I had never seen anything like it. It was an amazing sight and it showed all aspects of life in a funfair. Now, from my experiences in Ireland, where my foster sister would pinch money that I had got from thinning turnips and spend it at the fair in Wicklow, as far as fairs were concerned this had left me with a bitter taste in my mouth. I would sooner watch paint dry than actually go to one, but I had to prove to myself, and to be acceptable to some degree with the only mate I had at the time, by showing that I had outgrown all of these prejudices. I also needed to allow myself to have a bit of fun.

So, this weekend I headed out to Nottingham with Smiggy on his Ariel motorbike and me on an old 1953 BSA250. Neither of us would have ever doubted the reliability of the old 250 in getting me there and back without a problem. When you are young there are some things that you don't worry about and that you can do without turning a hair. You just expect everything to 'turn out alright on the night' and, on this occasion, so it did. As we strolled around and looked at all the wonders that the Nottingham Goose Fair could throw at us, two girls turned up and asked us had we got a light for a cigarette. At that time I did not smoke myself but Smiggy did, and he gave them a light. He then immediately turned to me and said we had best get going and, as we left the two girls, I asked what his hurry was. He informed me that those girls were too experienced even for him, never mind for me, so we made a swift exit. To this day I do not know how he weighed up those girls but whatever he saw must have been bad because he would not normally turn down such an opportunity so easily.

When I lived in Clay Coton I would often trip off to the Fox and Hounds pub, which in those days was kept by the Twynhams. Mr Twynham was an ex RAF guy with the typical RAF moustache and his wife was very fond of the odd gin and a game of crib. Some of the top business people in and around Rugby would spend many an hour at Clay Coton in that little pub playing crib. In those days it was more like a private little club than a pub. I remember one day when Mrs Twynham, who was getting well on in years, decided that she was going to learn how to drive and Mr Twynham had brought her a brand new Mini for her to practice in. On this particular morning she had pestered Mr Twynham to take her to town to do the shopping and so that she could get in a bit of driving practice. On the return journey home, as she was driving into the entrance for the car park by the pub, she put her foot on the accelerator instead of the brake and headed straight for a cess pit, demolishing a couple of apple trees on the way. She had most certainly made a mess of the apple trees but that was nothing to what she had done to the car! This, of course, was the talk of the area for months afterwards.

I would often find myself in the Fox and Hounds in those days, meeting up with the locals – the Boltons, the Shaws, the Sergeants and the Coopers and had many a good hour drinking nothing more than sarsaparilla. This took a bit of getting used to as far as the local people were concerned, as they could not get their head around an Irish guy not drinking Guinness, or even a drop of the hard stuff. They would often wind me up regarding this.

We would have a game of ninepin skittles with three cheeses, a game that was unique to Northamptonshire, Leicestershire and parts of Warwickshire, going back many decades. Everybody would have to take their turn in what they called the wood-yard and after the other players had knocked the skittles down you would have to stand them up again ready for someone else to flatten. I suppose, if you compared it with my last abode in Ireland, Clay Coton would not have been too far away in terms of being in a lovely country setting. Looking back I realise that I could have bought three cottages in this beautiful place for £3000 so I could kick myself now for not being able to make a move.

At this time, living in Clay Coton, I may have looked on myself as being a stranger in a new village, but it was very noticeable how quickly the village people and its surrounding neighbours took me in to their lives as if I had been part of it from day one. But it was to be many years before I realised what wonderful people they were. When you're young it is so easy to overlook the fact that people care about you and that they wanted you to be fully involved in their society. At this time I was beginning to realise that people must notice that there was a young guy not mixing that much with his own age group. For example, a woman from nearby Yelvertoft sent a message down to the Boltons that there was a trip going to Drayton Manor Park and I was invited to go with them. I doubt whether that would have happened in a city or a town where a young person could almost always go unnoticed. I was surprised to attract attention though, as I didn't understand that people could be so concerned that they would try to include you even if they didn't know you very well. So, I joined into as many things locally as possible, such as the village dances, the skittles matches at the Fox and Hounds, and the odd trip to various places.

Having my own transport – and with it a bit of independence – was always at the front of my mind and I had bought a BSA three-wheeler car which dated somewhere back to the 1920s. I had bought it with a view to doing it up, as the drive shafts to the sun and the moon planet gears were wrecked. It was put together in a bizarre way with an old type of canvas belting that they used to drive threshing machine pulleys but where they put the bolts through was plated over the belting. To make any improvements I had to get all that out and put plain washers over the belting, which was a difficult proposition, but it worked. One day I was determined that I would get the thing going. While I finished off some work underneath I realised that not only was this engine water cooled but it was also air cooled, which meant you would not want to stop too long in a standing position with the engine running as you would soon have the thing boiling.

When the landlady looked out of the window while I was working away underneath the vehicle, she thought a fog had come down as she was unable to see. Then she realised the fog was being created by my little three-wheeler car so she and her husband came charging over to rescue me before it blew up, as they were convinced that it would go up any minute. Well, I climbed out with the raucous noise that was going on, calmed them down and then they could see for themselves that the smoke and steam was starting to die down and they could all relax again – but it certainly gave them a bit of a turn. I ended up getting the thing to run again and I sold it for the same money that I paid for it, £15, after spending weeks on sorting it. I suppose you could say it was a useful learning curve in getting some practice in for what might lie up the road in years to come in terms of my transport

Many of the young men I knew at work, or at the boxing (that I had, by now, got back into – more of that later) or in the local TA, would end up with a steady girlfriend and I knew that Smiggy at that time used to try and groom me to prepare me so that a girl could see that I was half civilised and improve my chances of success. I would dream and hope that one day I would find a girl that I could get on with and she with me, without my worrying about stepping on her toes or kissing her goodnight with my crash hat and motorbike gloves on. There were times though when it looked like it would probably remain just a dream, that it was never going to happen and that I would end up not getting married at all. It just did not seem possible that it could happen for me. Obviously these kinds of thoughts could throw young guys' minds when they are in their late teens, and it becomes even more worrying when they turn twenty-one. Every year following that big birthday the situation becomes more concerning than ever, the doubts multiply and you start to wonder is your destiny to be a bachelor or could it ever be possible that you would find someone, get married, and have children? All of these things would be spinning around in my head and giving me grief. I think these worries were probably more common in people like me who had such an unstable background. I would always have doubt in my mind and would continually ask myself was the girl only interested in having a cigarette from me, or some way-out drink of her choice at my expense? Perhaps it's a good thing that I wasn't rich. If I'd had plenty of money my doubts would have been far bigger as to whether they were after my money or me, and there would probably have been a very good chance that my destiny would have been sealed. If I had been in that situation I would have definitely remained a bachelor. Despite all my worrying, at the time I had no idea how all of this would pan out. As they say, destiny is still unknown.

After many false starts in my social life (especially during my days at Parker's with my mate Smiggy) with regard to getting me matched up with a girl, a friend made a blind date for me in Coventry. My date was a very pretty and pleasant girl called Violet. The girl's family were very staunch chapel people and were extremely strict regarding what would be acceptable for their daughter in terms of entertainment. So, because of my inexperience, it was thought that I would be ideally suited to this situation. She became one of my first girlfriends. She was a lovely girl, extremely well mannered, and had a sense of decency about her, but I suppose when you are a young man you always want to choose the kind of girl you want for yourself, so this was far from being the perfect match I required. We used to meet at the weekends and we carried on like this for some time. It was then suggested to me that I would be able to sleep in the spare bedroom at her home so that I would be able to stop for at least two nights over the weekend. Everything was going fine and we were getting on extremely well, but I used to suggest that we could go to a dance or go and have a quiet drink in a pub; somewhere we could have our own space, but this was always frowned upon and was given a whiff of vulgarity. Her religious-minded mother seemed to consider herself morally superior somehow and was certainly not very pleased with those sorts of suggestions. She made me feel like I was suggesting something totally immoral for me and her daughter to get up to.

This went on for a while, and, as ever, there were other complications. Her uncle had a caravan and Violet was always wanting me to go to this caravan with her but I didn't wish to go because I was not ready for what might happen if we were alone for any length of time there. I suppose this didn't please Violet as she was definitely in love with me, or something of that kind, but I most certainly was not ready to go down that particular route. Of course, with not being able to go to the pictures, the pub or a dance, I became restless in my mind as to where the relationship was going. Don't get me wrong, many a guy that would have had the chance of going out with Violet would have thought himself very, very lucky. She was a lovely girl but with all these other obstacles getting in the way I seemed to have moved into a smoke filled cloud where I was not seeing everything as plainly as probably I should have been. I think that as I had always been so free since being a child to do as I wanted, I found it very difficult to comply with all these new rules and regulations. They were alien to me and I rebelled against them. So, at Christmas 1964, I suggested to Violet that, in order for things to work between us, her mother would have to agree that we were old enough and responsible enough to choose our own way without it being considered sinful, wrong, or anything else. If we couldn't get to this point, I told her, she would have a choice to make – be totally dictated to by your mother or come what may with what I wanted to do. I tried to explain to her that I needed to live my life without any restrictions from holy spirits or holy men. This was something that I was not prepared to be in competition with. At the end of that Christmas holiday she knew exactly where I was in this regard and I told her to think about it until Easter and that when she had sorted out which way she wanted to run she could let me know.

I took this stand then and was very sure of what I wanted to happen in that relationship but six months earlier I would have given my eye teeth to say that I was going out with Violet. And yet here I was, in a situation where I was turning down one of the loveliest girls you could ever have met. But, yet again, I suppose when this destiny man is working out your route there is nothing too clear to you as the victim. I have no idea myself whether it is clear to the man who works out destinies for people, but I most certainly have been confused more times that I can count. And at this point in my life it was no exception.

Of course, I waited for Easter. It came and went but I had no communication from the girl that nearly was my wife. We will see what destiny turns up for me in the fullness of time.

Chapter 5

Not all plain sailing

Life for me in England was often very difficult. I continually felt that I didn't quite fit in – although I sometimes didn't appreciate just how different my behaviour and attitudes were – and all my thoughts seemed to be dominated by the need to earn money to support myself and to help out my foster family. There were many trials and tribulations that were to hit me full in the face over those first few years in England as I established myself and, in effect, grew up.

As I have already described, a problem that hit me in the first few months of being in England was a nasty scare with my appendix that resulted in me having to go into hospital in Cromer, where I was on a trip with the TA, to have an operation. Life is never plain sailing for me and this was something totally new for me to cope with. But it wasn't all bad news. Whilst I was in

103

hospital – and out of my usual circle – I met some interesting people. One of the patients used to do portraits and he said he would like to do one of me. I agreed, but I did think that the poor lad had lost his marbles. My foster family did not visit me in hospital but this should not have been a surprise for me. They would usually be at my door begging for me to pay their bills but would always be absent if they were needed to give me any moral support.

The other patients, who I become very friendly with, had obviously noticed that nobody came to see me. As everybody else would have visitors, I stuck out like a sore thumb. They asked 'don't you have a girl friend who might come and see you?' and I replied 'no, I never had time for girls at all'. But the next evening I had the shock of my life when some of the TA girls turned up with flowers, grapes, oranges and chocolates and made a real fuss of me. Of course, my fellow patients believed I had been having them on and these girls turning up like this had actually made a liar out of me. They were not my girl friends, of course, they were people sent to visit me by the TA as they thought I might be in need of cheering up! I had a terrible time living that down as the other patients gave me such stick about those girls coming to visit. It gave me a totally unjustified reputation as a ladies' man.

That wasn't the only incident that caused me to be the subject of gossip and fun in the hospital. I used to lie watching TV in the room allocated to the walking wounded, and a nurse, in her own time, would come down and watch TV with us. No problems there but because it was getting cold and late at night, well past the time I was allowed to watch TV officially, she shared her blanket with me, and even that found its way all around the hospital. You would have thought I had committed a terrible crime the fuss they made about it. When I heard what rumours were going around the hospital about me and that nurse I was really embarrassed and as red faced as a skinned tomato.

Whilst I was in the Cromer Cottage Hospital there were a lot people affected by Spina Bifida who were associated with the hospital and there were also polio victims. The hospital staff put me in charge of looking after all of these people whilst I was convalescing and one time I had to have them sitting in seats watching a local carnival go by. My job was to make sure they were not participating in the event – they were only supposed to view it! I didn't mind the work but isn't it odd how embarrassing this could be when you are a young fellow. Coming from Ireland where the Irish society was geared in such a way that these cases were not normally mixed with non-afflicted people I had no experience of dealing with people affected like this so I felt even more exposed to the embarrassing situation. Nevertheless, apparently I did a good job and kept them all in order and God help us, there but for the grace of God go I. Of course, we should not be so shocked when dealing with these situations. People like this are part of our society and they should be made to feel so without causing any awkwardness to their own egos.

My extra time in the hospital came to an end and when I came to get dressed my trousers did not fit me because I had put on that much weight. I had been having two dinners a day, plus seconds should I need them and this made a huge difference to a young guy. I had been used to a diet for the last eight months of bread and jam so I had taken full advantage of the great food on offer in the hospital. I was also well pleased by how I had been treated during my time there. You hear about nurses being angels and my experiences at the Cromer Cottage Hospital bore out that belief out to the very word – they were brilliant people. They did not treat me as an idiot, they did not treat me as Irish, they treated me just like everybody else and that was a wonderful feeling.

On leaving the hospital they arranged for me to be put into a wheelchair and would not allow me to walk from the hospital to the ambulance. They took me by ambulance to the train station and then loaded me carefully onto the train. A big sign saying 'Reserved – no-one else allowed in' was placed on my carriage door. At that time there was still National Service lingering on and a serviceman was in the passageway outside my carriage, all dressed up as if he was joining World War III. Once we got going I beckoned to him to open the door and invited him to take a seat instead of sitting on the floor. He tried to protest that it would not be allowed because of the notice on the window, but I made it clear to him that if he wanted a seat he could forget the notice in the window. He accompanied me back to Market Harborough and then carried on his journey to London. For me he was good company and I could not see him sitting on the floor when I had a good seat and a whole carriage to myself.

So it was back to life in Market Harborough but it was going to take me a few weeks of convalescence before I could return to my work at the Grass Drying Plant. Whilst I was convalescing, my old mate Mike Smith called to see me and he had just changed his motorbike to an Ariel Arrow, which had just come out. It was a beautiful machine – one of the first off the line. If you had such a motorbike today the environmental people would have you locked up for polluting the country. It had a 2-stroke engine and the smoke it threw out was horrific. These bikes were like land jet transport. The discharge would fill the street in seconds despite the bike being brand new!

In those days there was no light work and if you were going back to the grass drying plant you either did the job or you didn't, but I can assure you it was not funny flying around on tractors a few weeks after having your appendix out and having an infection in the wound as well. Of course, in the summer if it was very dry you would be flat out trying to keep the tractors fully occupied gathering grass because of the dryness of it, but if it were very wet we would sometimes be in bed three hours before we should have knocked off, but this was understood. There was no dishonesty involved, it was just swings and roundabouts.

I always say that the British people are as good a people as you will ever find anywhere in your lifetime. That being said, I have had many disagreements and I was bullied when I first landed at the Grass Drying Plant. People would always be joking and clowning around but to some people I would be the eye of the joke. However, in many cases they would not be laughing with you, they would be laughing at you. Some people would happily call me a bogtrotter, which I have to say was something I was not amused by and I found it very narrow-minded thinking. Just because I might have been thick at that time would not mean that all Irish people were thick but that fact did not stop the catcalling and assumptions made by a few idiots that I worked with. Some of my fellow country-men were without doubt the backbone of British literature but, of course, as I had nothing myself to bargain with these arguments it would be nice when people like George Bernard Shaw would slip into the my mind, or some of the great Irish writers that came out of one street of Dublin. To my shame, I knew very little about any of these great writers but what bits I had heard in the course of my life to that date I think I put to good use in the arguments.

When the grass drying stopped we turned to other work on the estate, such as potato picking in acres of land that you could only dream of in size compared to what I had been used to. This gave some people the opportunity to continue their degrading antics and when they had the women on the potato machines they had great pleasure in taking my clothes off for their pleasure. One cannot imagine the embarrassment and shame of this situation. But, again, it is funny that no matter how bad things are there is nothing better than to overcome the situation. You just get on with it and hope the women were far enough away for them not to be embarrassed. This, of course, was bullying to a very extreme level and it was quite commonplace within both British and Irish society at this time. It was a common occurrence, in engineering for example, for apprentices to be humiliated for the pleasure of others. Another trick they got up to there was flicking spuds so that they would hit the rear target for a bit of fun, but when some people were hit they would be looking for the biggest spud in the field, or a rock, to retaliate. There would then be a bit of chasing the culprits until one or the other would give up through being out of breath. A lot of this larking about, or high spirits or whatever you might call it, would not, to a lot of people, be real badness. But, believe me, there were some people who were very poor at people laughing at them rather than laughing with them. This bullying didn't just involve a downtrodden Irish kid, but I did find the whole situation confusing and difficult to say the least. I had lived a life more or less as a recluse prior to coming to the UK and I found the whole thing totally mad and could not make any sense of where anybody was coming from. I would not even have considered it being bullied at the time, I suppose, but I would be clawing my way through the situation and trying to understand why this should ever happen to anybody.

Whilst we lived in Market Harborough, the house at No. 17 Leicester Road, which is now demolished, was next door to a children's home, and it is odd to think that I had grown up being so badly affected by this sort of organisation and yet there I was living right next door to one and not taking any notice of it whatsoever. One incident, however, did give me a rude awakening and a very severe jolt to make me aware of the children's home. I was coming back on my motorbike from Clay Coton to Market Harborough one evening when a youth jumped out in front of me. Luckily the brakes worked reasonably well on the old 1953 BSA250 but he almost had me off as well as nearly hitting him. I jumped off and asked him what he was playing at and if he was trying to commit suicide. He would have been a lad of about fourteen or fifteen and he replied that he was indeed trying to commit suicide as he lived at the Home and could stand it no longer. I'm ashamed to say that despite having suffered similar desperate situations, I was so tied up in my own life that I did not have the understanding and patience to deal with a young life that was so depressed. My reaction to him at the time was simply from my own angle rather than looking at both sides and I yelled at him that if he wanted to commit suicide I would prefer he picked someone else and not give me such a terrible fright. But now that I look back, yes the kid was stupid to do it to me and was inconsiderate getting me involved, especially as I was on a motorbike and was likely to get injured, but I do now have some guilty feelings that maybe I wasn't as caring and as understanding a Christian as I might have been. But then again, I am not perfect.

I think that when people are chucking kids into homes and into council care they need to be aware that their solution to the problem is not always in the best interests of the children. To think that a young lad like that should be so stressed and depressed from living within that environment that he was prepared to take his own life makes you wonder if the people running such organisations were a very long way short of dealing with it correctly. I suppose if I had not been so shaken up myself I might have been more involved in what had got him into this state in his young life. I'll never know what happened to him and I regret that. I suppose, at this stage in my development, I could not appreciate his problems and it is only when I look back years later that I realise that maybe I could have helped him and that I certainly should have been more understanding. I suppose my problems at that stage in my life were taking all my attention.

As I said, life was not straightforward for me but it was not without its rewards. My efforts produced results in various areas – boxing was one of these areas and, as it was very important to me, it became a bright spot in my life (although, as you will see, it was not without its disappointments) so I'll tell you more about it in the next chapter.

Chapter 6

Getting back into boxing

As readers of my first book – Hannah's Shame, about my childhood in Ireland – will be well aware, boxing was very important to me. It was the only thing that I had found in my young life that I was good at and it improved my self-esteem no end. But disaster struck in this area shortly after my arrival in England.

When I passed out on arriving at work on a frosty morning on a motorbike without my gloves (which had been stolen at the cinema the night before), I popped along to see my own doctor just to be on the safe side as I wasn't used to being anything but healthy. I'd regularly been travelling twenty-odd miles to work on my motorbike every day without coming to any harm at all but on this particular day I was, as I said, without my gloves and I was so cold when I arrived at the Grass Drying Plant that I passed out.

My doctor suggested that I went to the Towers Hospital in Leicester to be tested for epileptic fits. I had no idea what he was talking about and thought it was a fuss about nothing so I went along to the hospital without worrying too much about it. When they carried out the tests in Leicester, they placed a big net of stuff on my head – to pick up currents I supposed. They found nothing wrong as such but unfortunately they had come up with some theory that there was some characteristic involved which could point to epileptic fits. That being the case, they informed the Amateur Boxing Association doctor in Market Harborough that I was not ever to be allowed to box again and that my medical card had to be taken from me. (This was the Leicestershire, Northamptonshire and Rutland ABA – The Three Counties.)

So, the ABA 'miracle doctor', Mr. Swallow, declared me sine die in relation to boxing. You can't believe the shock and disappointment when I found out, at nineteen years old, that I was never going to box again. When I had decided to come and make a life for myself in England boxing had been a big part of my plans. I had come with the idea of

116

progressing my career in boxing and eventually turning professional in the sport so this was a real blow. It shattered my dreams. Nobody could give me a reason as to exactly why this had happened to me, which frustrated me even more. In life, destiny can never be compromised. How things can blow up and change, or come and smack you on the nose. This was an enormous blow to me at such a young age and, although I had only been training in Market Harborough and had not boxed competitively there, it left a gaping hole in my life.

At the Market Harborough club I had met some real characters and famous men of the boxing fraternity including George Adridge who was a former British and Empire Middleweight Champion. Also, it was the first time I had been exposed to the more organised approach to boxing where the whole thing was taken more seriously, which was a huge wake-up call for me as, when I had boxed in Ireland, I had got used to a very casual, laid back approach to boxing at this level with badly run clubs and a lack of regular commitment from all concerned. It was at Market Harborough too that I met Tom Jacobs who was a Shop Steward and who introduced me to trade unionism. Incidentally, his brother was an official in a boxing club and had been a professional boxer in his youth. Now, presumably helped along by the money he made in boxing, he had opened a large electrical shop on the square in Market Harborough. By a strange coincidence my landlady at that time was related in some way to the Jacobs. It seemed that although I had been told to stop boxing, I would keep being dragged back as I kept tripping over boxing connections like this.

But my boxing career was not to end there. As ever, more drama was to come. It was at the Grass Drying Plant some time later that I first met John Parker, an ex-professional boxer who had broken his arm in a motorbike accident at St. Thomas's near Newton, and this had wrecked his professional career. Although I had been sine die by the Three Counties ABA, he was always urging me not to give up but to have another go with a different ABA. Johnny Parker would keep reminding me that as I was now nearer to boxing in Coventry than I was to Market Harborough, or even Rugby, I should see about taking another boxing medical and he suggested a doctor in Yelvertoft. After the bitter disappointment of being turned down by Dr Swallow at Market Harborough I had no doubt that it would be very unlikely that another doctor would pass me fit, so I did not rush to make an appointment. It's odd isn't it that when you think that the answer is going to be no, you are very hesitant. You take longer, putting it back and changing your mind, but in the end you say hang it, I can only die once. I came to the conclusion that it was worth a try as I could only be embarrassed and frustrated with not being able to box when he tells me for the second time. As always, I was fighting my own thoughts as to whether I really needed to be told a second time. So I had all those things going round in my mind. Even if the doctor said yes I knew that I would then be wondering if it was the best idea – maybe I should not do boxing again; maybe it's in my best interest not to do it again. My eternal battle was going on in my head, one part of me wanted to do it and another part is saying the doctor said you can't do it – that should be enough, after all he is a doctor. So, one should not run away with the idea that it was an easy decision to go and take another medical to do boxing or not to do boxing. But the lack of boxing had left a terrible void in my life. Real success in boxing was one of the ambitions that I wanted to achieve. I suppose there was very little that I was good at and as I had become better at boxing than at most things it was all the more reason that one part of me was saying make sure you do it, don't give up, don't accept the normal advice that 99% of people would accept.

Anyway, I finally took up Johnny prompting for me to try again and see if I could box at the Woolpack in Rugby, which came under the Warwickshire ABA and not the Three Counties ABA. Despite my misgivings, I got hold of my medical cards from the Rugby Club and saw Dr. Stack. Now, wait for this! He passed me fit. OK to box! That was certainly a shock to the system. After the examination he told me he could find nothing wrong and, of course, I was very naughty, as I had not told him what Dr. Swallow had said, i.e. I was sine die. My thoughts on this 'economy with the truth' are that sometimes, in this world, you have to help yourself a bit. So fate can rub and turn and your destiny is certainly not predictable.

Johnny Parker was pushing me towards

boxing in Rugby. Of course, Rugby had been well blessed in the boxing fraternity over the years. They had had a very rich vein of talent with Johnny Williams the heavyweight champion boxing there, also the very capable Joe Leeming, a light middle weight, and then there was the very capable Billy Barber. Leeming and Barber, of course, both boxed for England. There would not have been many towns in the UK or anywhere else with the standard of boxing that they got from Joe Leeming and Billy Barber (who became an ABA referee and refereed some of my fights some years later). It is an odd coincidence that I had also lived in Market Harborough where Jack Gardner, a great opponent of Johnny Williams hung out. I have to say I feel very honoured that I have met all three of the Rugby people, plus Jack Gardner.

But, despite its former glory, the club at the Woolpack in Rugby was coming to the end of its days and on hearing of this, my new found 'family', the Boltons in Clay Coton, who I met in the Fox and Hounds pub, decided, at the start of the following season, that I should take another trip to Coventry but this time not to go so far into the city but to go the Willenhall Social Club in Robin Hood Road, and see what was on offer there in the boxing line. When I first went to visit the club I made some great connections including Stan Mannion, a man as proud of his cauliflower ears as if they dripped with gold or diamond earrings! No good going there if you were faint hearted – it was a tough club for sure. So there I was after this remarkable turn of fate, training at the Woolpack in Union Street, Rugby and, although I had been passed fit by the doctor, from that day onwards there was always a little bit of me not firing on all cylinders, as you might say, because of what was shrouded in the doubt as to whether I should or should not be boxing.

So, I never really put my heart fully into it whilst I was at Rugby Boxing Club but I continued to train, although there were no public contests arranged and the club was dwindling. Then we were struck with the blow that the trainer of the Woolpack was heading for Nottingham. That trainer, Jim Doherty, was an extremely proficient bantamweight. He had even boxed the great Terry Spinks and people who boxed him, as they say in Co. Meath, would have to be better up than standing. He certainly was the most skilful and tough opponent you would ever want to meet. He was from the north of Ireland and his departure from Rugby sounded the final death knell and although the club stumbled on for some time after this blow it was without any direction or purpose.

Incidentally, Stan Mannion was the trainer at Willenhall and had fought through the Singapore calamity. I didn't realise it at the time, but I had the honour of meeting a truly great soldier who went through that campaign, prisoner and all, but he was unrepentant, uncompromising, and would not know the word surrender. I met one of his trainer colleagues, John Toll, recently. John is now 75 years old and told me that Stan Mannion is in his nineties. How I admire that man. I feel so proud to have met such a great guy. He even turned up with the Willenhall gang at my wedding. Another character around at the time was Benny Roberts who was then the matchmaker and who has since passed on. Willenhall, Coventry, was one of the biggest working-men's clubs in the Midlands and had a gang of old social club members who could not do enough to promote the boxing group.

They would have their own tournaments on a regular basis and, of course, a lot of these members would have been Irish or had Irish connections.

After meeting these people I became a Willenhall boxer. I was proud then of the club and I am still very proud that I have walked the same walk and talked the same talk of that club and their officials which became part of me. These people treated me as if I had been their own son. At Willenhall there was no such thing as anti-Irish or taking the Mickey out of a thick Paddy. I was so happy at that club, where I stayed and boxed for 3 or 4 years. At this Club it was the first time that I had actually been in a club where you were made to feel important, and where you had all the facilities that were necessary. Even so, it still took me some time to take control of my boxing career. I kept telling myself that I needed to get a grip on the situation if I was to make any progress in boxing but other things, including the need to earn a living, kept interfering. Of course, working at the Grass Drying Plant was normally a seasonal job and people who were the most reliable employees during the summer and autumn, and those who had been known to the company for many years, would have had the first option to stay on for the winter months as they would find you bits and pieces to keep you going until the spring arrived. I was one of those who got extra work so this meant I didn't have as much time for my boxing as I would have liked. However, eventually my boxing career in England started to take off after all those years of stumbling along and not doing much or taking it seriously, but although I went on to box until I was 43 I don't think I ever fired properly and obviously was unable to reach my true potential after such a long break in what should have been my best years as a boxer. I suppose part of this delay was my fault. I should have realised just what was possible earlier on and taken up my friend, Core Bolton's offer of finding a club in Coventry. With so much going on in my life, probably one part of my mind was hardly able to believe that I could box if I wanted to.

Leaving aside my self-doubts and the fact that I had wasted time in the years before I came to Willenhall, my boxing career at Willenhall was successful and eventful. Stan Mannion, the senior trainer, was certainly a tough diamond and someone who gained respect, but he wasn't the only one a new young boxer had to impress at Willenhall. John Toll was fifteen years or so younger than Stan but if you were getting ready for a contest before you were matched, you would have to pass the test of John Toll and depending on how you did in that sparring situation he would decide on whether you boxed or not. I did well in the sparring sessions in the Willenhall Club training sessions and, of course, as I had trained consistently in the previous years without having contests because of the medical problems, I wasn't in bad shape. I may have always looked better than what I was, in terms of confidence, as the people I would end up boxing would have had the practical experience of actual bouts whereas I would have only had training without experience of a proper contest other than sparring. It would be difficult to match somebody like me under those circumstances because I was a boxer who had the experience so I looked, while sparring, as if I had been around the ring a time or two but was not really 'match-fit' so I was always going to be difficult to find the right type of matches to get going.

But the matchmaker did his job and my first contest at Willenhall was against an army selection team. I suppose the mere mention of the army selection opponents would have been enough to put me off my dinners for a week.

Mind you, when you think of how things are today in terms of sport, most good sports people, whatever sport they take part in, are very soon training full time but, of course, for people like me the same opportunities just were not there. I was working full time – from 7.15 in the morning until 5.30 in the evening every day – and it sapped a little bit of your strength to say the least.

But my biggest problem in the ring was me. My lack of self-belief continually got in the way. I suppose my background would kick in with all my doubts and lack of confidence. The non-belief in my own ability would render me to be in the 'B' team instead of in the 'A' team. I wasn't happy with the match-makers at Willenhall as I thought they were mad to match me with such quality opponents. It is only when you look at this further up the road with more focus that you are able to diagnose clearly what a dilemma it would have been for anybody matchmaking people like me after what I had been through as a child and youth growing up in Ireland. I also had had the saga of being sine die by the Three Counties ABA to add to the doubts that swirled around my mind continually. But what made the matchmakers' task so much more difficult was that a couple of days prior to the selection I would have been sparring with some of the best guys around and definitely holding my own against them. But for some reason my doubts didn't show up so powerfully in a training or sparring situation as they did when I stepped into the ring for a real fight. I couldn't believe some of the boxers I was being matched with. There was an ex-schoolboy champion and ex-junior champion of the ABA and, of course, to be fair to the matchmakers and officials – poor old Ben Roberts, Stan Mannion and John Toll – I must have been their nightmare because they knew, based on my training efforts, that I was more than capable of holding my own with anyone that they had matched me with and I suppose they were as keen to see me performing against the best as quickly as possible. Needless to say, in those days to me, as the guy stepping over the ropes, it did not always seem that way. But of course one of the biggest assets in boxing is confidence, and that was my weakest department and looking back now I can see for anyone matching me as a competitive boxer it would have been a real problem.

It wasn't just the trainer and matchmakers at Willenhall that would be able to work out that I could perform better than what I did. All of the people who came and supported the boxing on training nights would have no doubt that the right decisions were being made and that it was my performance in the ring that needed sorting out and that the problem wasn't bad matchmaking or anybody else's fault. There was one such supporter at Willenhall who had threatened me that he would stick me with a long hat pin if I was to get myself lodged anywhere near him on the ropes, and he also promised me that if I was to go down he would stick the pin in my rear end. I thought these people were mad, but looking back now I can see where they were coming from. They were obviously very frustrated.

There are no words that could express the enormity that this situation would have represented for somebody like me who had come through what I had done in my earlier youth. I suppose this would be a little bit different from dodging goats in the Wicklow hills as a wretched skinny half-starved kid. Boxing against some of the opponents being put forward in those early days at Willenhall for me would be like a step into Earls Court in London fighting for the world title, or five or six world titles altogether.

One of my first fights took place in Nuneaton, and I remember that Billy Barber, the ex-England International from Rugby, was the referee. My opponent threw a big right hand in my direction. I must have thought of the goats in the Wicklow hills so I dodged and danced like them and made myself scarce and poor Billy Barber, the referee, was flattened with the enormous punch that was aimed for me. Now, anything like that happening to a referee, or anyone in authority for that matter, for some unknown reason would always give me a great lift and I just could not stop laughing. But while I was laughing at poor old Billy Barber, my opponent got me clean on the chin and down I went. I suddenly thought of the Willenhall fan who had said he had this big pin so I got up off the canvas on to my feet and back into the ring in double quick time. On that particular night I stopped my opponent in the second round. This was, of course, a bit of a fluke in some ways but I suppose all this would add fuel to the fire in the matchmakers' way of thinking that if I could do it on that occasion then why wasn't I doing it more often? The way this fight went might have had repercussions with this particular opponent but luck had it that the lad's father, who used to follow his lad around to pretty much every fight he had, was on shifts. This was lucky for me because after that night he was always promising me that the tactics used on that occasion in Nuneaton could, if used again, result in me camping out on the canvas.

All the people connected with Willenhall who saw me perform in this way and grab 'glorious victories' were puzzled and frustrated by me. But of course they hadn't known my background and had they been able to read my first book, Hannah's Shame, it would have been an awful lot easier for them to understand. To be fair to them, they weren't on their own because no matter who I came across or socialised with could have come to the wrong conclusions about my character and my responses to others. I was carrying, after all, a great deal of baggage from my early years. I know that for me to be still boxing and still getting into a ring despite all these setbacks and all of the disadvantages that I had had to endure as a young boy growing up in Ireland, was quite something. People who weren't from disadvantaged backgrounds could not possibly imagine what it was like and although it was over four years since I had left Ireland, the impact of the past tapped me regularly on the shoulder, and would always bring me up with a jolt. No matter how much you fight it; no matter how much you deny it in your mind, the lack of confidence and the lack of education is in your face on a daily basis, and a lot of people could never have imagined that somebody like me, who now appeared quite outgoing and at the top of their game, as you might say, could be battling those demons. I think this goes to show that you should never assume too much about any young person that you might meet. They may have experiences locked away but unfortunately their locks are not foolproof. This baggage always has a way of seeping through, saturating and contaminating your very being.

Funnily enough, a lot of the supporters at the Willenhall Club were very proud of me, regardless of what I may have thought. After I boxed I would have people coming up wanting to shake my hand and saying how well I had done. I suppose they appreciated that a boxing ring wasn't a place for the faint hearted to be in, and they could see that I always tried hard and did my best. I was surprised to discover that there were people in the club who believed that, should I ever get into the right frame of mind, I was capable of achieving a great deal more than what I had already achieved. Again, boxing was doing wonders for my self-esteem – although those old doubts and insecurities never left me.

But no matter what you say, and no matter whether you win or lose in the ring, it was a tough old game with all of the other interfering factors in my life which would affect training. Once I was matched I always felt obliged to honour that arrangement and, of course, some of the time I would have been happier going to bed as I would have been so exhausted from one thing or another but I would not allow that to get in my way. Also, although I had no idea of it at the time, I was suffering with a blood disorder, and this would have been like tying your two legs together and trying to take part in a marathon. It was tough.

Time was rapidly flying by since I had moved in with the Chidlows. I had had a few bouts with the Willenhall Boxing Club – venturing outside the Coventry area and meeting people and boxing people in Banbury, Nottingham, and at the other Coventry Clubs as well. As I was in the Territorial Army the people that knew I was boxing for a club in Coventry informed me that they had put my name forward to represent the Leicestershire and Derbyshire Yeomanry in the Great Britain and Northern Ireland TA Championships. I might tell you I was not amused when I was told this had been done, as I quickly realised that this was a whole different ball game. The fact was that in the TA Championships of Great Britain and Northern Ireland you could meet some exceptionally good opponents and your club matchmaker, who, of course, was familiar with your capabilities and would usually only match you with suitable opponents, would have no say in the matter.

The dreaded weekend of the TA Championships arrived. It was taking place in the York TA Centre (this is now a shopping mall). As I went into the hall I came face to face with lots of people who were togged out perfectly, with 'business' stamped all over their faces. I looked around but could only guess as to which one I would be likely to end up fighting. I stood looking blankly into the crowd of strangers, hoping against hope that it would be nice if somebody would come and pick me up and take me back to Rugby before the hour of destiny arrived, but, of course, I had committed myself. My pride would not let me make the decision to turn tail and run, even though I was trembling with fear as to what might be about to blitz me off the face of the earth.

As boxers made their way from the changing room into the ring to fight in the TA Championships there was a fanfare blowing and all eyes would turn to check out the boxer. Believe me, that fanfare would make the hair on the back of your neck stand up. It was a very sobering experience and really made you aware of the enormity of the situation. What followed was always hard work.

The TA Championships started at 2pm on a Friday afternoon and would run through Saturday afternoon into the night, so you could end up boxing four or five times in the weekend, which I did on several occasions. In November 1964 I got through to the semi final and boxed some people far more capable than me and was classed in a higher category that I had ever been in before. I won through some rounds but lost in the semi final and felt a real sense of achievement. When you put the two things together – the hopelessness of my case from my early days in Ireland and that same lad taking part in the semi final of the Great Britain and Northern Ireland TA Championships – it is hard to believe that any of it happened.

But these weekends weren't all about just the boxing. As we were travelling away from 'home ground' there was always the potential for disaster or entertainment. One of my fellow lodgers, Stephen Walsh, from Kirkby Stephen, came with me for that boxing weekend at the York TA Centre, and we stayed at an army barracks in York. Stephen had planned that after the boxing we would go to stay for the rest of the weekend with his parents in Kirkby Stephen. Now, Kirkby

Stephen was quite a distance from York and after boxing and having a few wallops landed in my direction – particularly one or two on the bridge of my nose plus a few head butts in the face – I was not in the best of shape to undertake this journey. To make matters worse, a tremendous fog had come down and I was driving on roads that I did not know. But no matter how shattered I felt I could not let Stephen down – he was looking forward to seeing his parents. Stephen was an apprentice at AEI in Rugby and would only occasionally have a chance to be with his parents, so we persevered irrespective of the road conditions and we finally arrived.

Stephen's parents could not have been friendlier, or more welcoming to me if I had been one of their own sons. They looked after me as if I was a king, but insisted that I had to go to their club. Of course, in boxing there are a lot of unknowns that can crop up and bite you at any time, and although I had boxed four or five times over the weekend, I didn't have a mark on me. Stephen was amazed by this and had told his friends that I had boxed and that I did not have a mark on me. And he'd told them this not just once but four or five times – they found it hard to believe. Anyway, my nose was playing me up a bit and I blew it to get some relief. Of course, this was the worst thing I could have done as the veins in my nose were already damaged and blowing it fractured my nose. This resulted in two lovely, shiny black eyes. Black eyes notwithstanding, I had to carry out my visit to their club and felt highly embarrassed doing so! Oddly enough, although I boxed for thirty-three years I never had a black eye before or since this incident, although I have still got plenty of trouble with my nose.

I remember that Jack Gardner, a one-time contender for the British and Empire Heavyweight title, used to present the prizes at the dinner shows at the Grand Hotel in Leicester following these Championships and you always felt something special when somebody like him was presenting you with those prizes, no matter what the result and whether you won or not.

As I've already mentioned, Ken Bolton's father, Core Bolton later took me to the Irish Boxing Club in Coventry to join their group. For some unknown reason I never took to the idea of wanting to carry that out. I suppose one of the reasons may have been that I felt it was oversubscribed in terms of membership and I felt that I would not have been a priority in their scheme of things so I thought for that reason I ought to look for another club. Also it was right in the middle of the city and I was living in Clay Coton, Northamptonshire, so I really wanted a club much closer to there.

The amateur boxing season would start from the end of September and finish at the end of May, and at that time I was still quite fond of having a knock about with the hurling sticks that I had collected and brought over with me from Ireland. A gang of us would get together at Newbold Recreation ground, next to the Newbold Rugby Club and all the kids would have a great time playing this mad Irish game. I used to wear an old pair of boxing shorts for this knockabout and some of the guys would want to know if I used to box. A lot of them, including the Bales, the Ashwells and their mates, wanted to know why could I not start a boxing group in Newbold. Now, that was something I had never even thought about before but I was swamped with the enthusiasm of all these kids who wanted to have a go at amateur boxing. My first impulse was to say forget about it, it's all too complicated but I knew what I had gone through to be able to take part in the sport. Being a bit of a soft touch, when these kids were all wanting me to perform a miracle, I got carried away with their enthusiasm and promptly set about starting a boxing club in Newbold village. So, I made an appointment to see the vicar, Mr Miles, at the Newbold Church of England. I can see it all now – the graveyard and church were on one side of the road and the village hall was up a bank on the other side. Little did I know what I was getting into as I walked up the path to the vicarage.

Being totally inexperienced in this sort of thing, I allowed all the kids and young lads to accompany me to the vicarage. When I look back on it now I think we should have filmed it as it was unfolding. As the gang crowded into the vicarage it must have looked like a scene from the Pied Piper, but it certainly had the desired effect. The vicar was most enthusiastic about the plans and as long as we accepted his rules he had no problem in letting me use the hall for the purpose of amateur boxing training.

I must tell you here that, although I had never considered starting a boxing club or anything else – apart from the occasional hurling game – that would occupy the young lads in my area, the situation of young people and improving the facilities available to them is something that is very close to my heart. Even then, as a young man myself, I could see that this was a problem – a bomb waiting to explode. There were dozens of kids that were in the gang in that area and you can understand that when you have so many young people who are not occupied or able to express their characters there can only ever be one result – and that is mayhem.

I believe that instead of people like me having to go around rapping at doors to get people to give facilities to young people, they should be looking for people like me who have had the experience and the will to want to assist the society that we live in and help make it a better place for all. These sorts of facilities should be in every town, village or city for young people and then you would find that you did not need to be employing experts, chiefs of police and the likes, puffing out their chests as if they were great successes in what they are doing when in reality they all represent total failure and disaster. To make a difference we have to think differently. We have to accept that youth may all go and join a boxing club on Monday but by Tuesday a lot of them will want to join something else, and by the end of the week you will be left with only a small number who actually want to stick it out. You then have to wait for the next wave to come through the door. You need to be able to respond to that and to supply the skills to fill that void with the necessary interest for that type of young person. This is the only way to gain mutual respect between the youth and older people. Stop giving the lottery money to the operas and to societies that are very well off and give it instead to the areas where it is really needed. This situation and way of dealing with the problem is certainly, to my mind, a disgrace. Only when we are seriously committed to doing something for young people will we be able to sweep all that rubbish out of our way and concentrate on giving the facilities to the youth organisations so that we can clear the streets of crime and enable us to empty the prisons.

Of course, starting the Newbold-on-Avon Boxing Group meant a lot of effort. I had to go to see the then Mayor of Rugby, an ex-Liverpool City man Stan Carter. Now, he was a down to earth sort of guy and with his help we got the group going to start the new 1966 ABA boxing season off. We were up and running by the 30th September. But again, nothing runs smoothly for me. During this period I was a member of Willenhall Amateur Boxing Group. By starting up the Newbold-on-Avon Amateur Boxing Group I changed roles from being a boxer to being a matchmaker, secretary and trainer in one go. But I wasn't completely alone in my efforts. When you start something new it is amazing the enthusiasm of some of the locals and they wanted to play a full part in making things work – the News, Halls, Ashwells, the Burrells, and in fact Maurice Burrell even came on board to assist as a trainer fairly early on. Denis Hines, a Belfast man, and ex-Rootes boxer also came down to give a hand.

So there we were, up and running and we had nearly got a team of lads, particularly schoolboys, to take on the world as you might say. It is tough when you start a new club because none of your people have had any experience of having taken part in a real contest. The consequence of this is that you find the other clubs won't want to have a club like ours at one of their tournaments. Amateur boxing in Warwickshire was well established and there were a lot of clubs with a very long history of taking part in public bouts throughout the county. They could easily manage without us but we needed them if we wanted to box competitively.

I suppose it's a bit like the old gearbox because of the speed that the flywheel went around to engage the clutch – you had to build another mechanism so you could engage gears without ripping the cogs off before you got going. It may be a crude example to display to you, but the more I think about it the more it was like the situation that we had to deal with, being new in the Warwickshire boxing world. We had to bide our time and, with patience and perseverance, would get the odd lad on different shows. One of the solutions was for me to try and get fit again and start putting myself as available to box for the new

Newbold club as well as looking after the training and arrangements. This, and other little moves, helped to get people to book us when it was a very bleak outlook at the beginning, but I suppose a football player-manager would probably be in as good a position to know how tough it was to manage his own team as well as play for the same side that he was managing. Not easy. But when you are younger these sort of marathons are all taken in your stride and we started to get the lads matched all over the place by adding to our selection of youth boxers with senior boxers and people like Denis Lines also making a comeback. Gradually, we were starting to lay the foundations of a club that would run for many years. It's odd when you think, had I not been down at the recreation ground with the old hurling stick, knocking the ball about in boxing shorts, all of this would never have happened.

People forget now that anyone who was very active in sport in those days would also have had a full time day job to content with. Even for active boxers in those days it was commonplace to hold a full time job down irrespective of how tired you might have been at the end of a shift. Of course, today a lot of people are lucky and get sponsored by companies, sports councils or even lottery money. We used to complain about the Iron Curtain countries having the advantage over us because the sport was their job and that situation has now crept into all amateur sports in the UK and, for that matter, probably across Europe as well. I suppose in some cases it makes you wonder where the amateur ends and the professional begins. And with all of the drugs business to enhance performance going off, it is just another world today. If I were starting again tomorrow I most certainly would not want to have to be in so many different camps.

The sport of boxing is physically exhausting. It is difficult to explain the situation to people who have not actually done amateur boxing, or any other type of properly controlled boxing – but perhaps had only had experience of falling out with someone in a pub or somewhere. It is a totally different experience for someone to climb off the ropes and start exchanging punches with a person they had never met before. Being in the ring definitely sorted out the men from the boys because you would not be having the protection of the illusions that drink would give you, or the fire in your belly from being upset with someone who had just smacked you for no reason. In the ring you would have to be far more calculating and controlled and, as they say, you had to learn how to hit without being hit. But how much easier it is today to be able to get across a lot of the finer points of boxing skills to new pupils and to be able to point out to them their own mistakes by having a simple video recorder in the gym. You can learn more from seeing and having your mistakes pointed out to you in five minutes than you would have learned in a year without that assistance. I certainly wish I'd had a video recorder!

The first tournament that we ever had in Newbold-on-Avon was at a fete at the new Rugby Football ground. They organised the fete to generate funds for their club, and I staged the open-air boxing tournament. This attracted huge interest and whilst the boxing was on there would be at least one thousand people all around the ring trying to get a bird's eye view of what was going on. But the weather wasn't kind to us and I had to battle to keep the contest going. When you are young nothing could put a damper on anything. You can't even be defeated by the elements. Of course, having an open air boxing club in the British Isles, no matter what time of year, is a risky business and although in those days late May was usually warm you could also be pretty sure that there was a likelihood of a cloudburst sometime during the event. That's when I would have the run in with the officials, some of whom would be only too willing to call it off because of the rain or the prediction of rain. I had different ideas. I would insist that if a hundred people could stand around a boxing ring in the rain we were not going to disappoint them. That was my attitude and if it got too wet we would just have to have a sheet to cover the ring until we got a break in the clouds. So the show goes on. This seemed to me like the poor man's tennis. I thought that if the rain did not stop the Wimbledon tennis tournament I was not going to let a drop of rain stop the Newbold ABC tournament. I would say to the other officials 'Come on, we are in a man's world now, with Rugby Football and boxing'.

The other main problem apart from getting ourselves accepted and booking bouts with other clubs in the area was money – or the lack of it. But we had ways of sorting that problem too. A tote was started for example and people like Spud Murphy, an ordinary working chap, would have a fist full of tote cards and he always got them filled. These funds paid for the equipment that was needed as well as the everyday outgoings of an up and coming young Amateur Boxing Club. But again there was a tremendous amount of having to fight your corner, and, as I was not a person dead keen on dotting every 'i' and crossing every 't', I was often the target for the ABA committee to do battle with. But that came with the territory.

Our quest to raise funds for the club was helped by the way that the Newbold village people had immense respect for the Newbold ABC and all that it stood for, and that eventually spread to the people of Rugby itself giving us great respect and support as well. Some of the well-established Irish business-men of the area would be the first to put their hands in their pockets for a £20 note for sponsor money to help pay for a tournament or for new kit. Some of these great people have now passed on but I will never forget their willingness to support young lads in sport and wanting to make a difference in the society in which we were living. I mention the Irish connection deliberately but, of course, there were many English business people as well who were brilliant sponsors and without their help some of the tournaments that were staged would not have happened.

I don't believe that people in our society take on board seriously enough the great need to support young people who take part in sport. It gives young people a pride and sense of purpose that a good many of them would never have achieved without taking part in some kind of sport. Councils and governments, and the money distributors from the National Lottery, need to take this far more seriously than they are currently doing. With the 'concrete jungles' that are being constructed all around us there is a bigger necessity than ever before to face up to the need and the responsibility that we have, as a society, to the generations that are to follow. If there had been more people in a gym somewhere, or on the football fields, willing to give their time and experience to youngsters it could have saved the country millions of pounds in trying to keep them out of trouble and out of the jails and young offenders' establishments. It doesn't matter how much the politicians and people in charge talk and dream about eradicating this problem using ASBOs – this will just create a society of young people believing that the only interest older people have in them is giving them stress. Of course, I only feel so strongly about what I am saying because of my own personal experiences. I was so lucky that I ended up being involved in boxing and that it saved my life from being wrecked by crime.

In 1967 I had arranged for a boxing tournament to take place in the British Legion in Newbold. But I didn't get to this point without a tremendous battle with the ABA to get clearance for this tournament to take place. After a great deal of debating as to whether it was a suitable venue for an amateur boxing show they finally gave in and permission was granted. Two officers had been sent out to check the suitability of the hall and I will never know to this day what happened, but they cleared it for the show to take place. Somehow they had got the OK.

This night of the tournament in March was very cold so we had to have the paraffin blowers to generate heat in order to keep warm. Two blowers were placed near the entrance so that the heat would blow up the hall. Unfortunately, we had forgotten that some of the ladies wore dresses or skirts for these events and some of them would have their clothes blown over their heads! Still, it's all entertainment!

My confidence in the boxing ring always suffered more than most. Obviously, almost anyone would be nervous prior to boxing but because of my previous experiences I would have been more naked in this department than most others. The trouble with amateur boxing, particularly for people like me, was that I started work at 6.45am and finished at 5.30pm five days a week, and very often would also have worked from 6.45am until 2 or 4pm on a Saturday. That would be a normal working week for me. So I would have to rush home, have a wash and a bite to eat and then go to the rendezvous point and pick up the lads that would be boxing in the various tournaments, in places up to one hundred miles away. There wasn't much time left for error, and sometimes some of the lads would be late, or worse still did not turn up at all and didn't let you know. I found this attitude very frustrating then. I would have to say that, even now, 30 odd years later there would be no way I would be able to cope with it. I would blow a fuse to think how people could have such a laid back attitude when they had already committed themselves to a particular date. But isn't it funny, when you are younger you take all this in your stride. You say what you have to say and then just get on with it.

I remember I went to Banbury with my very good old friend Jim Cannon. He was a Donegal man, a down to earth sort of character who would never say a bad word about anyone. I worked with him at the Tile Works and we became good friends. He was the guy who kept the interlock tiles properly cured and was very committed to his work. He looked after the mixing of the acid that burned the colour onto the tile as they passed by on the ropeway, and it was this acid that would cause the wire to have frayed earlier than could otherwise have been expected. His other job would be to make sure the tile trucks were all in place, by the ropeway, for the operators to pass the tiles from the ropeway onto the trucks to be taken out into the yard to be stacked and left to cure before they finally ended up on a lorry and eventually on somebody's roof.

Jim Connor had done this job for many years. He was never unhappy at his work – he was always whistling or singing a Donegal song. How he managed to do that I will never know because most people would not be able to breathe because of the fumes of the acid, but it never bothered him at all. Jim had left getting married until the more mature time of his life but eventually married a lovely lady from an island off the coast of Co. Kerry in Ireland. Unfortunately, they were not together for very long but they were probably far happier than most people would have been. I will never forget Jim. He was always a good friend to me.

When I boxed at the Winter Gardens in Banbury some people that I knew were coming in late. I took a little bit too much notice of them as they arrived and, while I was distracted, ended up catching a punch which assisted me in seeing Blackpool Illuminations some 160 miles away! I remember they gave us a clock for a prize that day. In those days you got a prize whether you boxed or not as long as you had agreed to the match. I put the clock on the back compartment in my little mini and Jim and I were heading back to Rugby when I suddenly had to brake hard. The next thing I knew was Jim yelling and screaming because the alarm clock had hit him on the head as it flew to the front of the car. He maintained afterwards that he had had a worse experience in my car than I had in the boxing ring.

By this point in my young life I had met the girl who was to become my wife – more of how we met later – and we were very busy and happy at this time but Carol did not like the boxing much. However, she always loved to go to the Belgrave Working Men's Club in Leicester, and many a good night we had there. Carol liked going with Charlotte Bolton, Robert Bolton's mother, and some of the girlfriends of the lads that were boxing. The ladies would always go for a little walk if things were not going too well in the ring. There was a bonus at the Belgrave as they served black pudding with peas. Carol had become quite addicted to this dish. She did go to other venues but she could take them or leave them and always considered going to the Belgrade to be a little treat.

Carol and I were part of a large group of people with whom we became extremely good friends. It didn't matter whether you were boxing against someone in the group or were boxing another opponent, you were always held with immense respect. Boxing was, as you can no doubt tell, a very important part of my life. It brought me lots more good times than bad and, above all, it built up my self esteem to levels I would never have thought possible. Of course from my previous experience as a young child and as a youth growing up so isolated in Ireland I often found that some of the heartfelt fondness and respect that these people had for me was an embarrassment, as I had never experienced this sort of treatment. As a result of my performances in the ring there would be so many people wanting to shake my hand, and the club officials from the female side would want to kiss me. My goodness, how I am talking you would think I was a Casanova or something, but believe me by the time some of these people had finished kissing and hugging me I looked like Coco the clown and would be plastered with lipstick and powder.

I can assure you I didn't really welcome a lot of this attention. At the time I would be most embarrassed by it all and I would often take evasive action if I saw some of the female officials coming in my direction. Carol, of course, would be gob smacked by all this attention coming my way. I suppose she often thought she couldn't let me loose on my own but there was never anything like that in it; they were just so friendly and great people. There was one particular lady who had a heart as big as a bucket and I will never be able to explain it, but as soon as she spotted me she would be after me like a setter. She was very liberal with the lipstick and powder. It would be like a wrestler's embrace that she would lock you in to. But when I look back I think how embarrassed I was, and how it took me some time before I could settle down under this barrage, but wasn't that a long way from being excluded from society as a child and as a youth? What a change. Who would believe that someone who only had goats for friends as a youngster had now met people who were prepared to give such love and respect. When I look back I can see that I almost took it all in my stride. I certainly didn't dissect it. The experience of growing up unwanted set against my experience of being a young man who had found another life in England was amazing.

When you went boxing in those days (and I believe the tradition has carried on today), there would always be refreshments for you, and even if you didn't box you still got them. The thing was that when you were boxing you would not be able to eat your proper meal before going in the ring, so these refreshments were very much sought after and, in most cases, were of the highest quality as clubs took a pride in treating their visitors in the best possible manner.

It's funny, but at the time you don't realise how involved the whole set up was, how much you depended on other people and other people depended on you. I built up a reputation that I would never let any club down. If I gave a commitment the club knew that they could hang their hat on that commitment. Going around the clubs became a part of my life, and I felt part of an organisation. I wanted to play my part and to have had the respect that I got at every level was something I could only have dreamed about.

Some time ago I was interviewed by John Florence on BBC Leicester radio about my first book, 'Hannah's Shame' and an old boxing colleague, Karl Gunns, had apparently heard that the interview was going to be taking place. This interview was in 2006 and I hadn't had any contact with Karl Gunns since the late 1960s, as he had gone down a professional route and I had stuck with the amateur scene. It is breathtaking to know that the immense respect that he had for me and he wasn't content to think it, he went to the trouble to express his warmest respect by phoning in to the programme. These are the sort of friends that I made in a career that spanned 33 years. I have to say I feel extremely proud, and very lucky, that I can go many miles in any direction from the Midlands and find great respect from the people I have worked with. They were some great people and anyone who had met them would have to say how lucky they were that their paths had crossed. Although it's hard to let go when you have been involved in boxing for over thirty years, in the glowing twilight of your life you still have great memories which nobody can take away from you.

Chapter 7

The TA

Not being able to take part in boxing at the Market Harborough Working Men's Club was a terrible blow to someone of 18 years of age – to think that my career was over before I was even twenty. It was a tough situation to be in. I obviously needed something else in my life and the TA was a lifesaver at this point because it occupied some of my ambition, which I was not to fulfil with boxing. Some of my spare time and energy was taken up with going to camp in different parts of the UK and that must have stopped me brooding about the lack of competitive boxing in my life. I was also occupied with the different world that the Territorial Army had allowed me to enter. Having to mix with more than one person at a time was a totally new experience for me and the emphasis on personal presentation drove me mad. I had never had to worry about polishing boots or pressing clothes before in my life, so it was certainly an education for me.

I was very lucky in finding my way in to the TA. I had nobody to advise me but I would certainly tell any young person in my position today to do exactly the same thing. I think a young person setting out in life – and especially going to a new country – if they are ill equipped, ignorant and without education like I was, would be well advised to get involved in activities like the TA and, of course sport. These activities enable young people to make friends that they would not otherwise have had, and can overcome any lack of skills such as mixing with other people.

As I have said before, to many people my joining the TA would have seemed to be a bizarre move. I felt I had broken away from slavery and I hated snobbery and the TA would have had a lot of the things in it that I had great difficulty in handling. For example, being ordered around, being shouted at, and having to salute anybody senior in rank – comics in some cases – would have been something that I really railed against. All these things would have been foreign to me but they taught me some valuable life lessons. When you consider what I had been through as a young child, boy and teenager in Ireland, it left me in a position where I did not make friends; I would have been a loner when I arrived in England but being involved with the TA and boxing helped me in undoing my depression to a point where I could open up my character like a flower in the morning sun. With the TA, I had to learn how to do things in a uniform fashion, to learn how it was to be governed by time and to be smartly turned out. All these sorts of things, in a strange way helped me to overcome mountains of differences that I would have fought against every step of the way. In short, it helped me become part of the society that I chose to live in. Oddly enough, this beneficial effect carried on. Further on up the road, even after I was married and had my own children, being in the TA helped my children going to school, being accepted more easily into the society in which they lived. However, I can assure you none of these benefits would have crossed my mind as being important, necessary or anything else, I believe that it was simply destiny taking over and where it unfolds you just have to follow.

Of course, in this sort of regiment – the Leicestershire & Derbyshire Yeomanry – were the leftovers of a bygone age from the lancers of the 17th and 18th century regiments, where the officers were normally from the upper crust of life and would have batmen to serve their every need. This would, of course, make this environment an unlikely one for someone with my background but I suppose life is not simple, nor is it a perfect science, and people like me often ended up joining British regiments. We were the backbone of some of the British Infantry Regiments, as thousands of these unwanted children who grew up in Ireland were very welcome when they 'signed for the shilling' as soldiers. Some of them undoubtedly made extremely good soldiers but there were others who found that the contradiction in getting their freedom and then having to obey orders for a second time in their lives became too much and there have been some very tragic outcomes in this regard. For those who managed to reason with the contradictions that they were faced with, the TA and the Armed Forces in general helped them become more at ease with themselves and also helped them to become more, for the want of a better word, 'civilised', and able to deal with other people and with society.

It is amusing to think of me going into this environment. When I went into the TA I was used to dressing in rags and thought that polish was only used by posh people. For me to be faced with a situation where you had to bull your boots, use Brasso, and have all your clothes pressed with creases like razor blades, well, it's hard to work out how I coped with this bizarre set of circumstances. But I suppose at the time I would not have realised how much of a misfit or how much of an oddball I was. I know that I didn't take to these circumstances kindly or intelligently. In those early days in England I met people who were able to penetrate my prickly skin and my nakedness in terms of being affected by what they said and did. All of this was fermenting away in my mind when I was called up to go to camp in Cromer, Norfolk. As I said, it was like a new world being with so many people around, having to dress smartly and having to have your boots so clean you could see your face in them. It put me in a situation where my inner soul was having a battle royal with my inner demons as to why I should put up with all this rubbish – and volunteering for it at that!

As described earlier, things did not go to plan when I was at that camp in Cromer. I ended up in the hospital there, having my appendix removed. Being in hospital was yet another new experience for me and I certainly took advantage of the benefits such as good food, plenty of company and new things to see and learn.

During my time with the TA I went to plenty of camps and travelled to many different parts of the UK. For instance, there was the Lulworth Cove camp when we went on the train from Market Harborough in the boiling summer heat with all our kitbags and battle dress (which was like material made of briars), changing in the underground with the sweat pouring down our faces. Of course, when they told me we were going to Lulworth Cove they didn't tell me that this was a tank training camp. My face when the tanks started firing shells off at six in the morning must have been a picture! Everything around us was shaking and it was as if World War Three had started without anybody telling us about it.

Other camps that stick in my memory were in the Brecon Beacons in the Abergavenny area of Wales, Washington near Gateshead, and Barrybudden on the east coast of Scotland. You could not say we could get bored with going to the one place; there was always something different happening and I had started to make friends with people from Alfreton, Leicester, Market Harborough and numerous other places.

I failed my lorry-driving test at Lubenham Aerodrome, which is now Gartree Open Prison. In those days you could drive a lorry just with having passed a car test and as soon as they knew I had passed my car test they had me driving lorries to camp and back as well as on exercise, regardless of my failing the lorry test. But, of course, that took away my other travelling options of either going by train or in the back of lorries where I had no responsibility of having to get there, which was a bit of a disadvantage from my point of view. After two weeks or so driving lorries, when I got back into my mini after camp it was like sitting on roller skates. The vehicle I had been used to for a fortnight had suddenly changed to a little box on wheels and it would take some time to adjust. The old

Morris and Bedford lorries were very heavy and cumbersome, but in general terms were very reliable considering some of the hardships and rough terrain they would have to go through. Driving those lorries was one situation where my background in Ireland came in handy. On some of the exercises we went on, when a road vehicle would have to go on soft land, my experience on the farm gave me the advantage over the 'townies'. They would be amazed at how I would set about getting the stuck lorries out of the mire, and as I hadn't long since passed my driving test they found my performance very hard to understand. That would have been judging the situation from a townie's point of view and not taking into account that I had been through the agricultural university of muck up to the neck!

It's only years later that you find out that after they read about my achievements in the TA Championships in 1964, and saw the photographs in the Clifton Tile Works magazine (the Tile Works was where I was working at that particular time), they were all proud that one of their 'oppos' was making these sort of splashes. I think they were especially proud as this was in the sixties – one of the best decades in history. This was a time when ordinary people such as the Beatles, Cliff Richard, the Bachelors, Val Doonican, the Rolling Stones, Mohammed Ali (known as Cassius Clay at that time) were the celebrities of the day. And, of course, the awe for some of these characters has not diminished one bit and has, in many cases, gained more momentum. People remember them and many have become legends in their own lifetime. This was the background to my little bit of fame. Yes, this all took place in the year they were getting ready to take a trip to the moon and back. If you had told people prior to the sixties that this would happen they would all have said you had gone mad and would have booked a Black Maria for a journey to a more secure place for you.

It was a challenging and changing situation for me to be in this new world and I always felt that I was running to catch up. Throughout all my wonderful experiences – and bad ones – with the TA – I would always be wondering whether I had a family or whether my mother was still alive or my father and, if they were, where were they? I was always pondering whether people like me would have had relations. It was always on my mind and, of course, I would wonder if I would ever conquer getting the right girl that I would want to settle down with or whether that would just be for other people.

Of course, being in the TA you had certain responsibilities and demands upon you, such as two weeks at camp, six weekends away and one night a week attendance at the Drill Hall, but I enjoyed almost all of it. One of the biggest events was always the Armistice Day Parade. Now, I wasn't a tarmac soldier, so having everything to the standard required, i.e. boots so you could see your face in them, gaiters and belts Blanco-ed, all of your brass cleaned with Brasso, and all the creases in the right places, was a nightmare for people like me who had always been used to being in rags and up to my neck in muck. You could say this was one huge change to my constitution, and, of course, I had never used an iron in my life for pressing clothes and ironing shirts, so I had to find a way around that little dilemma. In the end I had to get some of the lads who were good at that to do my ironing, but I would have to repay their efforts ten-fold. I used to clean their boots and Blanco their kit and tack for them, and then do guard duty for the privilege of their help with the bits I was just useless at. But I was so proud standing in Market Harborough Square on Armistice Day when all of the different organisations showed their respect to the fallen in two great wars. We even had the Yankees, as then there were quite a few American camps around the Market Harborough area, and they would join in the proceedings. Of course, the English lads would always be going on about how bad they were at drill, but for me I had two left feet anyway and this drilling business was quite a pain, but they normally stuck me somewhere out of the way so as they didn't have the whole unit trip up and fall over. I could never get the hang of keeping in step and I must say whenever I did keep in step I didn't really have any idea that I was. I suppose if you have got two left feet you have got two left feet and you can't change that but I could never see that keeping in step when marching enabled you to do your job any better. The logic of that idea escaped me altogether. It seems funny how some of them, particularly the poor old sergeant major, would get extremely worked up over this situation. To get through this I suppose in most cases I simply closed my eyes and just hoped that either I did it right or nobody noticed that I was doing it wrong.

When I look back on those parades in Market Harborough or at De Montfort Hall in Leicester, it is odd that I was able to take to the principle of the thinking so easily and knew so much about the casualties of these wars that had taken place. My knowledge came partly because of people like Paddy Doyle who had known virtually every battle that had taken place since the Battle of the Boyne up to the 60s and would be able to tell me the different graveyards where some of the fallen had been buried, particularly in Co. Wicklow, and the history that surrounded these sites. I suppose for a fellow like me who didn't have anything in the world to hanker on about, other than my own country, it gave me a sense of pride to think of those brave lads who have passed on.

Being a part of the Territorial Army was certainly a great experience for me and helped me to grow up and to learn about life in a very enjoyable way. Although my life was changing at this time, my foster family were ever-present and caused me plenty of problems as you will see in the next chapter.

Chapter 8

My family problems

During good times and bad, wherever I was working, and whether I was boxing or going on camp with the TA, one constant in my life was the need to help my foster family. They were always there and always struggling to survive and I always felt that I had a duty to bail them out of whatever bad situation they had got themselves into. For example, when my foster sister continually wanted me to help her because her husband had failed her in his responsibilities, I always had that stress of deciding whether I would ignore her pleas and concentrate more on my own ambitions of buying a car and getting the deposit for a house or give in and help her. Of course, being the soft idiot that I was, there was no contest. Their problems would always win.

The funny thing about it now is after all I have done for all of them, my foster brother and my foster sister have as much interest in me and my wellbeing as they would have interest in having the plague. I suppose I eventually woke up and realised that this was for real and not just a game we were all playing. It takes many years for it to hit home for people like me to, as they say, wake up and smell the coffee. I now have to accept that there was never anything between us in terms of love and affection. There was only the convenience they had that I would assist them in their need to get out of a situation. That was all that would ever matter and nothing else.

I have to say that I have heard about this sort of thing since. I have seen stuff about problem families on TV and I have read about their problems, but you can never quite believe that this could happen to you. Somehow I was able to ignore what was staring me in the face and simply keep helping out, without ever realising that it was always one-way traffic. I would always believe that if I was ever in real need then they would be there for me. It is a tremendous shock to the system to realise that the whole of the early part of my life with the adopted family, the Donaldsons, in Ireland, was a complete sham and I will never be able to find words that could properly explain my feelings about this. I cannot bear to think that I went through a large part of my life believing that we would die for each other, but the reality is that none of it is what I believed it to be. This realisation was certainly a shock to me and I find it very sad. I feel sad not just because there was nothing between us, I also feel sadness for them because if they are so shallow, and so selfish, it just shows you the damage that was done to my foster brother and foster sister in their childhoods. The neglect and the conditions that we all had to endure couldn't help but have an affect on any child but different children are obviously affected in different ways. This should be a lesson to society that if you don't give proper care to children when they are young most will grow up where they have no respect for any-thing or anybody and that is a bad situation for society. It is a sad fact that very few will grow up like me, naïve.

Of course as well as the boxing, the TA, and working, my 'emergency services' would always still be on demand for Molly, Sean and my foster father. Also my two aunts,

Daisy and May, in Ireland would require my help so I would still have to do my best to contribute to their survival. Apart from assisting with daily expenses such as bills I also helped out in trying to make them more able to fend for themselves. For example, whilst I was in Market Harborough I paid for a motorbike for Sean in order to make him more mobile so he could find a job. That should have sorted one problem for me but life never seemed to be that simple for me because Sean's character meant that he would not just rest with having a motorbike, he would want to do the impossible and try and ride it after he had a belly full of beer. Yes, you have guessed it, he crashed and ended up breaking his knee, which only added to my desperation on earth in terms of trying to fund him.

I've tried many times to fathom out why Sean was as he was. What made him rely so much on my help when really he was more than capable of fending for himself. This is particularly strange because here was a guy, an extremely clever person, probably one in a million in terms of brainpower. As a youth and a young man, if he went into a dance hall, or wherever the ladies would be, everything would just stop. He had that appeal to the females; it was simply like a magnet pulling the whole thing to a halt. He was a very good-looking guy and had a charm that was astonishing. In complete contrast to me, he had many friends whereas I found it difficult to make friends and could not match him in any way. They do say that there is a fine line between genius and madness. I would think Sean would be a tremendous example of that saying.

As far as having common sense was concerned, Sean had none, but in terms of having brains to 'do' people and 'twist' people, plus the charm to come across with it, he was an expert. People would be lending him their last penny and be happy to do so, only to find out later the chill of their mistake and, of course, Sean would not even blink knowing how he would have taken the butter from their bread without them ever realising it. He was completely without scruples or a thought for anyone else.

I often wonder now what happiness he found from a situation where all his mates, who were the wrong sort, would cling to him like bees to a honey-pot. He was the sort who would attract them and he would be able to feed the situation and make it glow. He seemed to love the attention and was always chasing a dream. This was again in complete contrast to me. My own ambitions, rightly or wrongly, were always simple. I basically needed a roof over my head and enough to eat, and I would have been happy with my lot at any time. I never had that desire for the big palace or to live up to a status way above my realistic achievements. I don't know why we're so different and so damaged, and I never will, but probably some of it was to do with our background. Although my foster brother was not suppressed in his impoverishment as a child he had a very inhuman, uncivilised background – the same as I had myself – but he was always treated differently because he was their son and therefore he was not expected to do the toiling that I had to do as a child. He was not treated as a slave in the family.

Whether his childhood was the reason he felt that he needed to get his own back on society for allowing that to happen to him is questionable but it is the only explanation that I can find that would square the picture. For my own situation, I was suppressed as well as living in poverty and it left me in a state of mind where I would not have those burning ambitions to want anything grand. So, although you can have three people in the same situation their reactions will vary simply because we are human. Life and destiny are totally unpredictable.

From time to time it would be brought home to me just how bad things could be with my family, despite all my efforts. When I found out that my foster brother had broken into the store at the garage where he was working it was hard for me to believe that he could be so bad and so stupid as to risk the good job he had there. I was so shocked and ashamed. I could never express my sheer horror at the news, especially when you think that so many people would have given their eye-teeth to have landed such a good job. But there you go. All of this you can never explain, no matter how much you push it around in your head. I always came back to how could he let himself down, as well as letting everyone else down?

When the police came to arrest him and were questioning him he asked them if there was anything he could do to make sure they did not tell me about it. He was more concerned about keeping it from me than from his poor old father. The police, of course, told him not to worry about me. They said the courts would deal with him and they hoped he might learn a lesson. I suppose that must have made him feel a little bit more protected compared with what he may have thought my reaction would have been. In fairness to the police, they were very reasonable with him. Unfortunately, in this case, the civilised and caring approach from the police did not work and he most certainly did not learn a lesson.

At this point I was tripping backwards and forwards from Clay Coton to Market Harborough and also I would have had to travel to Hallerton, the village where Clarke had moved, when I would have to take some money for Molly to pay the electric bills and so on. Every now and then we would take a trip over to Ireland to see my foster father while he was there convalescing from TB, and to see my two foster aunts, Daisy and May. In the meantime I would also send them a few bob to assist them with their everyday needs. Neither his daughter nor his son sent them a penny whilst they were in England and their father and great-aunts were in Ireland. I suppose it took my foster father a very long time to realise that it was not his blood son that cared a damn about him but it was the unwanted wretch that he had fostered all those years ago that had an immovable sense of duty to assist them in any way that he could. I suppose, as a father, it must have been one awful dilemma to have to get your head around.

While I was working at Redland Tile, Sean had, as I mentioned previously, smashed himself up on the motorbike that I bought for him and this created a very bad situation as he was living with his sister Molly and brother-in-law George Clarke. I knew that he was a tearaway, and, as a consequence of this accident, was unable to work so what I discovered when I went to visit should have come as no surprise. When I went over I found that he was sleeping in a car parked outside the new house in Bath Street, Market Harborough. He had moved from the place at Hallerton because, of course, that being a railway house and as he had now packed in working on the railway, he was unable to live in the house and had to move. The money situation wasn't getting any easier, which always brings the worst out of people, and they were all arguing because he was not paying his way. He, as you might expect by now, would be very happy collecting off other people rather than them live off him – he was just a headache and giving to others wasn't his policy. When I found he was living in the car, my mind, stupidly and naively, went into overdrive again to see how I could help him out of this situation.

There was a woman who lived on the other side of Windsor Street, Mrs Rose, who took in lodgers. I went to see her to see if it was possible to get him digs there whilst his broken knee got better. Yes, you have guessed it, I also paid for these digs for many months and, of course, when he got a bit more able to do work I got him a suitable job at Redland Tiles in Rugby. It was a cushy number keeping the records for tiles, which would have helped give him time to get his leg fully healed. That went on for some months but when you are young, isn't it odd how all these things are happening and it seems to be like years, whereas all these changes are taking place in the space of just a few months. Despite the fact that I had got him a job, and digs in Windsor Street, he wanted yet more from me. I had got myself a new car and he believed that this car would be very useful for his requirements and for lifts at nights. Although I was never happy letting him – or anyone else for that matter – have my car, I did lend it to him for a night and wouldn't you know it, the petrol pump burst. In all honesty, this was a blessing in disguise because it gave me a good excuse to say that he was damaging the car when he went out in it and therefore I wasn't having any more of it. I suppose to be fair to my foster brother, the breakdown had nothing whatever to do with him and I had it repaired under the guarantee. But you could be assured that it probably saved my car from being wrapped around a lamppost a little further down the line so that faulty petrol pump may have saved my poor mini, which lasted me ten years.

But, alongside my family's problems, I still had my own demons accompanying me in terms of trying to find out who I was, and whether foster children, or adopted children, could ever have any relations. I was still determined to leave no stone unturned in tracking all that down. Yes, I have to confess that I was addicted to it. I would think back to my childhood and I was always wondering where my own connections had begun. I yearned to know who I was and whether I would ever complete the search for my own true identity. Although all the other activities that were flowing and bubbling around me occupied most of my time, effort and energy, I still had not have given up the idea of searching for my beginnings. But it would be a long time before I found out much in the way of useful or satisfying information.

Chapter 9

Looking back

Throughout those early years in England, I still made the regular trip to Ireland to see my two foster aunts, Daisy and May, and it gave me a great sense of fulfilment to drive up the road to their house in Dunganstown, County Wicklow, with food for them, and fuel for the fire. Since I had come to England I had been out of touch with that way of life of having to go to the hills and sawing down some bushes before you could boil a kettle of water. But getting back now and again to see my foster father when he had returned there and the old aunts, Daisy and May, was obviously very special to me because it was the only life that I had previously known. He was the only father I had ever known and I would have felt a lack of duty should I not have visited him and the aunts, but, of course, whilst I would be back in Ireland all the memories would come flooding back.

There were memories of the cold, freezing, wet days on the hill with a bushman's saw, cutting down bushes and having to carry them back to make the fires so that the tea could be made. I remembered with happiness the baking that could be done providing there was money to buy the flour. And there were memories of being in the hills running after the goats; being with my thirteen turkeys and their mother; stooping down and picking up my Chinese bantam hen and talking to her as if she was a human being. Being in the hills in the summer and being tired from the timber felling and then lying down in the heather to have a snooze, having my peace shattered by Aunt Daisy shouting 'Derry, where are you? In the name of God hurry up, we are dying for a cup of tea'. And then she would tell me that one of these days when I went to sleep in the heather that a lizard would jump down my throat and then I would be sorry for myself. Of course I feared that these lizards would multiply in my veins. I would often wake up in the boiling sun with the sounds of the corncrakes, grasshoppers, curlews and pheasants in my ears, and I would be desperately checking to see if there had been any lizards running about. These would be the both sad and happy memories that would flood back.

One memory that stays with me still is my longing, as a young boy, for a pair of long trousers. Readers of my first book, Hannah's Shame, will be familiar with this desire of mine and may even be waiting to hear how I went on in my quest for this elusive article of clothing. I remember well my foray into a shop when I was nearly fifteen. Dressed in my rags, I had been desperately trying to save money so that I could buy my first pair of long trousers. Oh God, how I longed to be able to do that. How I longed not to be in rags and not to be hungry. Anyway, as I was approaching the age of fifteen, having saved my money up from thinning marigolds, turnips and beetroot on my knees in the fields, there finally came the excitement of going to Fleming's store in Barndarrigh and asking Mr Fleming could I have a pair of long trousers. But nothing ever ran easily for me, nothing was ever simple, and I could never have believed what he was going to tell me. He said he had no long trousers for me and I asked him why not. He replied that I wasn't big enough for the ones he had. I told him that I knew some of the other lads were a few years younger than me but they were in long trousers years before me. He explained, very patiently, that they purchased their long trousers in the Wicklow town shops where they had a bigger selection of young men's trousers. After all the struggles I had had to get to this point, at this juncture my not being able to buy a pair of long trousers was not an option. I had news for Mr Fleming. I informed him that there was no way I was leaving the shop without a pair of long trousers regardless of whether they fitted me or not. And nor did I. I could not wait to wear the trousers and it bothered me not a jot to think that I rattled around in them and they were far too big for me, but that made no difference. I had got what I desired at last.

These were the memories that would flood back whenever I visited the Hill House, Dunganstown. But it was always great to get back to Ireland and to smell the turf fires and see the old haunts that I knew as a child. Apart from the memories and the sheer pleasure of being back, there was also a strong desire to find my real family, my true blood family, and relations as well as other little mysteries from my childhood in Ireland that I was desperate to solve. Who was the mystery woman who used to follow me, when I was about four, screaming for me to be given back to her? Of course, I would always use the opportunity of being back in Ireland to try and further my early childhood wishes of trying to find my family roots, and all that goes with it. When I started in 1967 I had no idea that I would be still doing research into my early roots into the next century. But once you start on a journey of this nature you become addicted to wanting to know more, and although I got to the end of that session and tracked down both sides of my family eventually, I am still shocked at what I am uncovering to do with my beginnings. The only thing is it doesn't get any softer, or any more civilised. If anything, the research involved in getting this book out has turned out to be even more horrendous than the research that I did into my first book, 'Hannah's Shame', which I did not think could be topped.

Although I always knew that the deprived life that I had as a child and youth in Ireland was sectarian based, it has taken me over 50 years to be able to read in an Irish newspaper (the Irish Mail on the 26th October, 2007) any admission of guilt from the Irish government. They were, finally, publicly accepting a report from journalist Ken Fox – who had the courage to tell it as it was. I have to confess that it gives me great pleasure and a feeling of enormous pride for a non-educated person like me to have had the success of having one department of the Irish Government, i.e. the Ministry of Health & Department for Children, to start to wave the white flag. However, they were quick to pass this particular hot potato over to the Minister of Education's department. The Ministry of Health maintain that the Ministry of Education was responsible for all that went on in homes such as the Bethany home, where I was abandoned as a baby. But it is odd, isn't it, that the 101 documents that I have recovered in connection with this all would have come from the archives of the Ministry of Health. It just shows you that even when the game is up these senior civil servants are unable to be honest and just say yes, we were wrong. What they are now trying to do is to build a smoke screen of confusion between themselves and the Ministry of Education. But surely they all know that in the end there is only one outcome to all this and that is to own up to the truth and do the right thing. They must now treat fairly all the victims of the abuse that took place from 1922 up to the most recent years. That can be the only way to wash away this dreadful stain that blights the Irish flag and embarrasses those who still have immense respect for their country. Of course, it is only fair to say here that the people in these departments are sometimes working under enormous pressure. Although Ireland pays lip service to 'Human Rights', the reinforcement of these rights is very badly funded so there are few staff to deal with the volume of work and issues can be dealt with in a less than effective way.

But a resolution to this problem can only be achieved by treating all abused and marked children equally. This has to be irrespective of what home they went to or what laundries they were enslaved to. It is no justice to only give it to chosen homes – the ones that had the most vocal input to civil servants and ministers. Nor is it right for justice to be based on groups that involve large numbers or just one religion. There must be justice for those who weren't in that position. Justice must be done so that Ireland can rid itself of the grave crimes that the state allowed to be carried out in its name by religion-obsessed men and women who were playing God with babies', infants' and toddlers' lives. This tragedy will haunt Ireland until the day of judgement unless addressed in a civilised and fair manner.

We must also learn lessons from the past and be aware that it is so easy to repeat this nightmare that we have just come through where unwanted children are concerned. The figures for the year 2000 for unwanted children in Irish care is becoming alarming again – over 6000 in a population of four million people! To put that statistic into perspective, if that was equated say against the British population of sixty-odd million you can clearly see that the gap that is starting to emerge in the Irish Republic in this respect is serious. It is something that there should be firm action taken on now to redress this problem before it starts to shame us again. Steps must be taken now to stop whatever is causing this to happen in Irish society. I was horrified to read these statistics in my research and it made me so sad to think that very little has been learned in all the years since I was a child.

Now, I don't think that I have the solutions to all the problems in this respect but I do know that there must be more done in the education of young people to make them aware of their responsibilities in relation to unwanted children. It must be made clear that is their duty to look after their own offspring and not the duty of the state or others. The state, in turn, should make it possible for this to be the case and to do everything necessary to cut out the cancerous thinking of churchmen that continues to lead to thousands of kids being cared for by the state or others. This is purely a creation of society and it can be one way or the other. It can only be right that people who bring children into the world do their duty.

But back to the search. Of course, returning from holidays in Ireland we would always have had some trails to follow and some information to exploit. Sometimes I would not deal with it immediately on returning home – it could take weeks or even months before I started having another push at seeking out the truth of my existence. Readers of my first book will recall that I started my search for my mother using vague memories of place names that I had overheard adults mention in gossip – as they do when they think children are not listening. One such place was Ardee and here I met an old lady (after going down a lot of blind alleys and many days of fruitless searching) who was able to produce a photo of my birth mother. Looking at a photo of my mother – it was of her wedding to an RAF officer – for the first time was a shock, to say the least. Now, I had no wish to cause my mother problems in the life she had built since she had given birth to me but, of course, it was important to me that we met. A meeting was arranged with her at Victoria Station in London through a go-between. My mother turned out to be a refined lady of the type I had lived among in my childhood – the ones that never gave me a second glance or a second thought in terms of helping me out of the awful situation I was in. I got the feeling that on this occasion she would like to meet me and then go and never look back but I couldn't let her go without asking her many of the questions that had been festering inside me for so many years. She calmly and coolly told me how she had been sixteen when she gave birth to me (although I later found this not to be true) and that members of her family had pushed her into abandoning me. It was difficult to ask the questions that I really needed the answers to – such as who my father was – so we parted with many questions unasked and unanswered. I was devastated when my mother refused to meet me a second time. She took the view that what was done was done so there was no point to taking this difficult relationship further.

Needless to say, I felt differently as I was desperate to find answers to everything that had bothered me for so long. So, when we were holidaying near my mother's home in Dorset, I took the chance to pay her a surprise visit that was not well-received by my mother. She did, however, agree to meet me later that week. I discovered that I had two half-sisters and that my mother was quite a socialite. But she still didn't tell me who my father was. I had many more telephone conversations with my mother over the years but the calls were always made by me and her lack of interest and effort often upset me. Eventually, she told me the identity of my father but then dropped the bombshell that he had died some years before. She also informed me – cruelly, I think – that he had expressed the wish to see me before he died. I'm convinced that she delayed telling me until it was too late for me to meet him and it makes me unbelievably sad that she denied both of us the chance to know one another.

One piece of helpful information my mother did give me, however, was that her maiden name had been Leinster (whereas I had always believed it to be Linster) and this led me to my grandparents. I learned that Leinster was often spelled Linster so that was where the confusion came from. This was a breakthrough for me and I eventually met many of my relatives, who were, without exception, wonderful people. They welcomed me with open arms and even expressed their shame at my having been denied a normal family environment. And this, of course, is the real tragedy. Being with my relatives made me realise just what I had missed and that there was nothing in this world that could compensate me for that loss. The real tragedy of my childhood wasn't just the poverty and the hunger or the lack of decent clothing; it was the total lack of love and affection. What I had really missed out on was having a family who cared.

My mother also laid to rest another thought that had haunted me for many years in my childhood – and since – and that was that my mother was not the mystery woman in the fashionable hat who had followed me and screamed for me to be given back to her. That still left that little mystery unsolved. Although finding my mother had been a lifelong goal of mine, I found it very unsatisfying. She was distant and kept to herself many of the things that I was hungry to find out, so my search for the truth about me and my roots went on.

Incidentally, as readers of my first book will know, I did eventually solve the mystery of who was the woman who had been following me when I was small. I finally persuaded the Social Work records people to put me in touch with a family with whom I had been fostered when I was only seven and a half months old. The lady's name was Mrs Shirley and, although she had died and I was an adult living in England by the time I eventually tracked her family down, I was lucky enough to meet her son, Tom. I went to visit Tom in Ireland and he was able to fill in many of the gaps in my knowledge of my childhood.

Chapter 10

Moving jobs

While research about my background, going on TA exercises, boxing and helping out my family were all important to me, the need to earn a living was even more so. I was continually looking to make myself more secure and to make sure that I could make a decent life for myself without relying on other people. Early on I had managed to buy myself a 1960 250 BSA Sunbeam scooter and my ambitions were still to save up enough money for a deposit on a house. I had always had the idea in my mind that I was going to buy a house of my own come what may. The funny thing about this is that at that time I had no idea how much a house would cost, or what getting a mortgage would have meant, or what the legalities and problems might be and so on, but being young, these sorts of things would never have crossed my mind.

What had started to cross my mind was that I had heard I could get a few more pennies an hour working for the Redland Tile Company at Clifton near Rugby. This was also a more secure job than what the Grass Drying Plant would have been, where seasonal work always meant that part of the year you had to look for casual work or hope that Parker's could find you a few odd jobs for you to do to fill in the gap during the winter. The Grass Drying Plant employed a lot of students, and it obviously depended on how things went as to how other people stood with regard to their employment. Of course, these students were only using this employment as a stepping-stone and a convenience to enable them to get the education that they were after. I remember one lad who was there during the summer who had a motorbike for transport coming from Rugby. He would be out all night at parties even though he had to work the next day and he often fell asleep whilst riding his motorbike and ended up in the hedge more than once.

I suppose, from my perspective, working at Parker's was a lovely, open-air job, and driving the tractors and operating the machinery was like home from home for me. In contrast, Redlands Tiles would have been a very dusty, dirty job and far more boring than what I had been used to at the Grass Drying Plant. But ultimately you have to make decisions – do you want a job that you like or do you want the one that allows you to earn more money and which also offered security during the winter months? I would have had to weigh all of this up and it was never easy for me, but I did want to better myself so the choice had to be for me to go where I could earn the most money, irrespective of whether I would have preferred to stay in a different type of environment.

So, in 1962, I moved to the job at Redland's loading tiles onto lorries from stacks. It was an outside job (which obviously I preferred to have) but it was very dusty and a tough old job throwing up tiles onto a lorry all day and every day. In the summer you would have the sun blazing down on you but being young I took it in my stride. In the winter you would have the snow and frost, and all the elements to contend with, which was not funny or pleasant but I was paid a few more shillings for doing it, and normally I had a little bit more security over the twelve months. Some of the lorries I had to load in those days were from big companies while others were one man bands and there was a variety of types – Brindley 6-8 wheelers and some ten tonners for example. The contractors drawing tiles out of the Clifton Works included Brindley, Dunkley's, Oak's and Robotham's.

I wasn't at Redland's long when a position came up there for a machine operator to fill hoppers with sand and the different coloured granules for the tiles. I applied for the job and got it straight away and I was over the moon because I loved driving tractors. The only trouble with this particular job was that if you lost your concentration and you let the hoppers run out of sand you would be in serious trouble. There were also other problems with hoppers because some of the tile sheds had different colouring in the granules and you were kept on your toes because you would not have had many seconds between each hopper running out before you had to attend to the other and when you were putting different coloured granules into two different hoppers it would be disastrous to put the wrong colour in or to let it run out. I certainly learned to concentrate.

We were heading for one of the worst winters in my memory – the winter of 1962-63. At this time, I used to get the Redlands bus in Clay Coton when the weather was bad (on this morning it was too slippery for me to take my scooter to get to work and the snow was too deep on the road) and then the bus would go on out into the villages to pick up other lads for the tile factory. I remember one morning it had snowed quite heavily and there was a very icy wind blowing. I had been waiting for the bus from 5.15am until 5.30am and thought I ought to walk up to Yelvertoft to see what had happened to our lift. It's a morning that I will never forget.

It started to sleet on top of the snow and then it literally rained ice and, of course, I would not have been properly dressed for such a dramatic change in the weather and standing around waiting for the transport to come was not a pleasant experience as the wind cut right through me. In the end I walked to the bus driver's house in Yelvertoft where I learned that because it was so cold he could not get the engine to start. Others had gathered by this time and we decided to walk to Redland's at Clifton. We could not walk on the road as the snow was blowing off the fields, so we walked along the hedge on the inside of the field to get to work. We eventually managed to get through that horrific nightmare but that period was the longest period of frost in living memory.

Some time later, when the roads opened again, Hayward, the van driver, had got up a bit late one morning. It was a very foggy morning and he was trying to make up a bit of time. We were heading for Cotesbach village but a milk float was slowing him down. He obviously had made up his mind that he had to overtake the milk float regardless of what the danger might be. Considering that you could not see a hand in front of you, the danger was certainly unknown. As soon as he overtook the milk float he crashed head on into an oncoming car. It was one awful bang. I got flung out through the side of the van and could not believe that, after I could start breathing again, that I was not in the van. When I looked over to where the van was it had only one of its back doors left. Yet one more road accident that I had been involved in – and survived!

Also involved in the accident was an Italian

chap called Fangio who was a great character and used to work on mixing the colours for the different tiles. He was the kind of chap who would be most annoyed – and would let me know about it – if I dozed off and gave him the wrong coloured granules, as it would render all his work useless and he would have to start all over again. My God, would he not tell you off with a string of words that you had no idea what they meant, but you certainly knew he wasn't best pleased! When I looked over and saw him sitting behind the driver he looked dead, and I certainly thought the driver was dead. So the ones who had managed to get out of the van were concentrating on getting these two out of their trapped positions in the van. When you looked at the area of where the smash took place it was just like a bomb had gone off. There were bodies everywhere and the most woeful groans that you had ever heard in your life. Oddly enough, when we went to rescue Fangio he was soon back at his best and he had strings of words coming out to express his dissatisfaction with the whole situation. We struggled and eventually got the driver out. Throughout this time he had been completely unconscious and we assumed that we were only releasing him so that he could be put into a coffin but, again, a miracle seemed to have happened – he had come round.

There was another lad involved whose name was Brian Shaw; he had a nickname – Bubbles. The poor lad suffered badly with his nerves. He was one of the best and an extremely hardworking lad who would never harm anyone, but he was a person who attracted people taking the goat on a non-stop basis. But Brian would always take this in his stride. Anyway, as we staggered about around the scene of the crash, we heard a fuss further down the road under a pile of metal. On further investigation we could see that this pile was one of the sides of van with the roof on top and Brian was in the middle sandwiched like a Swiss roll. As we pulled him clear, the only thing he was concerned about was that we were going to be late for work that morning.

But that wasn't what was on the minds of the rest of us as we clambered around, inspecting the damage and the injuries. We found one poor chap who was from Welford – Jesse we used to call him. Now, he didn't have a lot of hair left, but the accident had even taken a swathe of the bit that was left. There were moans and groans and blood everywhere. As I inspected the damage to myself I found that I had two big lumps cut out of my head after hitting the road and I was aware of the impact of my chest hitting the road and it winding me. There were broken collarbones, arms and legs. We certainly looked a pitiful, motley lot as they were putting us into ambulances and taking us to the Royal Infirmary in Leicester.

Some of the lads were very concerned for the nurses when they went into the bay where I was in being attended to. The nurses were trying to get my boots off and were using scissors to cut my laces up. Even though we were in a pitiful state some of the younger lads were cracking up with those nurses having to deal with my boots. Of course, that accident put quite a few of us on the sick for a while but we could only be very grateful that none of us were killed. It was an awful experience and they reckon we were doing fifty miles an hour when we passed the milk float. The car was estimated to be doing forty-five miles per hour when we met. I was off work for several weeks with my head wounds and was only offered

£223 compensation from the Redland Tiles insurance company who were, of course, responsible for the bus and its driver. Nevertheless, as I had never seen £223 before, I had no delay in quickly accepting the offer. I was told afterwards that I was very silly to have accepted it but I was quite happy with what I got.

I started to make new friends and meet new people when I worked at Redland Tiles. One of the new mates that I had made was an Irish lad from Kilkenny; his name was Bob Graham. Bob could not understand why I had buried myself away in Clay Coton and was always advising me that I would be better off getting digs in Rugby. At the time it made more sense that I did that and he asked his landlady, Annie, if she would take me in as well, as she used to keep three or four student lads and some lads from Ireland. I then made my decision to move into the big town of Rugby, which, of course, was enormous to me after living in the country for most of my life (apart from the little spell in Market Harborough) and soon I had moved into 47 Windsor Street, Rugby.

Annie was a Scottish lady who was getting on

in years and her place wasn't like I was used to, where the landlady would always have a dinner on the table for you when you got in after work. The idea at Annie's was that everybody looked after themselves and we only had the bathroom and the kitchen for our use, but being young this never really mattered because we would never have sat in at night anyway as we would be out until bedtime. I have to say that it was not my cup of tea, as I had got too used to Mrs catering and so I felt that maybe I hadn't made the right decision as far as this digs business was concerned. But, as they say, you never know what is around the corner, and funnily enough Annie was related to the Jacobs in Market Harborough. Tom Jacobs was the shop steward at Springer's Engineering plant where I worked when I first came to England, and his brother had an electrical shop in the square in Market Harborough. His brother also had a lot to do with the amateur boxing group in Market Harborough, so destiny is a funny old thing and it keeps popping up when you least expect it and everything turns upside down. The outcome of destiny's predictions is nearly always breathtaking, and never ceases to amaze me as I journey through life.

During that hard winter of 1962/1963, whilst I was working at Redland Tiles, they had coke braziers all around the sand to stop it from freezing and every spare hand was involved in preventing the frost taking over. In the end the frost was so severe that the sand would freeze going up the conveyor belts and freeze in the hoppers no matter how many braziers were put around it. Eventually the tile-making factory at Clifton had to stop completely as all of the water pipes had burst and everything was frozen solid.

This wasn't good news for me. I had just moved into my new digs in Rugby and I was not aware of any unemployment money or anything of that nature, so had no choice but to live off my savings or find another job. Finding a job was going to be extremely difficult as most people were experiencing the same sort of problems as we had. There were thousands of people being laid off throughout Britain. Of course, I was not really aware of what was happening. Under these circumstances you seem to hide in your own little world and were unaware of how serious the whole situation was.

Although I'd moved into Rugby, I was only seven or eight miles away from my old friends and I had kept in touch whilst at Redland Tiles with most of the people, and some for many years later, such as the Boltons. Before I moved to Rugby, whilst I was living in Clay Coton, I had heard of a farmer who might be interested in someone to help with odd jobs on the farm so I went along to see him when work finished at Redland's. One of these odd jobs was mucking out his sheds and cow pens, a job that had not been done for a long time, and that kept me going until the end of March, although it was a nightmare of an experience getting there and back because of the state of the roads. To a lot of people that would not have been a very pleasant job, but to me it was a few shillings that I would not have earned had I not taken the opportunity.

Most certainly the winter of 1962/1963 was something that I will never forget. There was far more snow in the winter of 1947 than what there was in 1962/1963 but the frost lasted much longer than in 1947. Also the snow that was in the fields blew onto the roads in the strong winds, which made travelling a very difficult experience and on some occasions I had to abandon the road and take a short cut across the fields in order to avoid the snowdrifts. But again, as they say, nothing lasts forever. The weather eased up and normal temperatures prevailed, which meant we were able to get back to doing normal things and resuming our more usual work patterns, so it was back to Redland's.

It is odd that when I was working at a roof-tiling factory I didn't really take on board what was happening in the rest of the industry. It's really part of the building industry and, of course, during this period all the building sites were shut down but at the time I never gave a thought that that could be a factor in the problems at Redland's. So, even if the frost hadn't stopped us directly we would have been stopped eventually because they were unable to build the houses and would have had no need for the tiles that we were churning out.

My life was seriously changing because I was mingling and living as a townie as you might say, which was a totally new experience for me to cope with. Bob Graham, who was working at Redland Tiles before me, had a string of cousins and relations all over the Rugby area and some of them were in digs with Annie at 47 Windsor Street. There were Tom Williams, Gordon Williams and Robert Williams, to name a few, who worked in the building industry for Richard Williams, who was their first cousin and had started his own building company. He employed them as well as other people but these were a group of young guys who had come over from Ireland in the late fifties/ early sixties with only one thing in mind and that was to better themselves. Of course, unlike me, most of them had served some sort of apprenticeship and all of them had a decent education, but one thing we did all have I common was that we weren't over here for any handouts. They all worked extremely hard and earned every penny that they made. They weren't expecting council houses or the like. They earned their own money and bought their own homes or, in the short term, like me, they paid for their own digs.

Tommy, for example, would be working for someone else for an hour or two before he started work for his cousin for his normal daytime hours and then he would do a few more hours' overtime after finishing his regular hours. An easy life did not happen for any of them. They had to work extremely hard for what they got. Although these lads were all Irish and came from an area close together in Tipperary and Kilkenny they didn't just stick with their own as you might say; they mixed in with the natives and some of them ended up marrying local girls. They weren't all perfect, but then again who is? They certainly taught me a few things that I should never forget in my life. They all achieved some of what they set out to achieve but there were some things that I could not take to. They would like their drop of the black stuff, which, of course, I could never see the attraction of. Despite the drink, all of us were very careful about spending money, and I would have been no different to any one of them in that particular area. I've heard it said that some of them could peel an orange in their pocket to avoid having to share it. I think one or two of them could have taught me how good they were at that and how I might have learned a thing or two on that score!

Robert Graham had ambitions like the rest

of the lads. He always had it in his mind that he was going to emigrate to Canada. Now, you often hear lads say what they are going to do but it doesn't always happen but I suppose that particular aim was one of the reasons why he was more careful with spending than even some of his cousins. One thing sticks in my mind about him – Robert Graham was a complete genius when it came to adding up. There was a lad, Michael, in the same digs with us who was still at college and when it came to adding up stuff he would be going to his bag to fetch out the latest technology available but, of course, Robert was something else. He would have the answer to the question or puzzle before Michael would have had the thing set up. He would be extremely annoyed with the fact that the Irish navvies would have the answer out before his wonderful new machine had even started.

I was aware of the ambitions that the other lads had – to go to Canada or to succeed in property and business exploits – but I was content in my own world. I had accepted that I did not have the education to achieve great things. I was more concerned with getting my boxing back on track again and I was not smitten by the desire to get rich quick. I suppose now that if I had given a tenth of the time that I had spent in the boxing world to exploits of trying to achieve business dreams I would probably have been better advised. But, then again, knowing my disadvantages, maybe it was a good thing that I was, as you might say, easily pleased with my lot.

I suppose the Irish capacity for adapting to circumstances is one reason why they do so well no matter where they go. Don't get me wrong, they love their own environment and having the craic as they say, but that wasn't to the extent of ignoring the social fabric of the environment they had chosen to live in. I suppose that is one reason why whenever one of them passes away you will find standing room only in a church because of the immense respect they have earned in their new society over the years and the audience would be mixed right across the spectrum of that society.

Life carried on at the Tile Works but things don't stay the same forever and by this time they had started to do the extension of the M1 motorway from Crick and of course the talk of all these great jobs on the motorway would be buzzing. Some workplaces were cleared out of labour almost overnight to take up the new challenges of building the extended M1 North. I suppose there were good opportunities, which I might have been better looking at more seriously rather than worrying about having a permanent, steady, but low paid job at Redland Tiles. But I was happy enough. I did what I wanted to do.

I had started back training for boxing by this time and joined the club at Willenhall near Coventry, after spending a year or two at the Woolpack in Rugby so that all kept me occupied, but Bob Graham and Johnny took their chances on the motorway and decided they would go for broke. They went to work for a company called Wixworth Quarries. As I've said, Bob was a very calculating person in terms of expenditure and he would have done his sums so I'm sure he would have been convinced that he would be more likely to achieve his main target of getting to Canada this way. He had a brother in Canada, well-established as a vicar, and it would not have been such a huge ordeal for him as it would have been for someone like me who would have had nobody to go to. The Williams and Graham families would have had relations in virtually every English speaking country and it would have been like going from home to home. Of course, I would have found this very difficult to understand, as I did not have relations anywhere, or at least I didn't know of any then.

One winter I worked at Tungsten Battery factory in Market Harborough which was like, in parts of it, pulling a curtain back and going into the 18th century with the beginning of the Industrial Revolution. In one side of the factory they made the bits and pieces that went into the lead sections of the battery cells and there was a big wheel with gas flames underneath it, to have it glowing red. The wheel had pillars where you put copper pins in to what would form the battery terminals. Of course, when you bought a battery, you would not realise that some uneducated idiot of an Irish boy had left some bits of his fingers, which had been melted by the hot metal, in this roundabout mechanism. On the other side of the factory they made the batteries and assembled all the bits. Some of these batteries, which were massive, were for the Post Office, which at that time included the telephone services for the whole country, the Army, and so on. The smaller vehicle batteries were made at Tungsten's in Market Harborough. In one area of the factory there was a fog of acid in the air and the first time this fog hit you it was as if you would die coughing. Remarkably, I met an Irish guy who had been working in there for 40 years. During this time he had certainly lost his countrified complexion and this had been replaced with a pasty grey look.

By this point I had traded in my Sunbeam 250 BSA twin scooter for a brand new mini car. But having a new mini always had its drawbacks. One, I was terrified of it getting a scratch and two, I was always having to run people around in it as if I was a taxi driver and had shares in the local petrol station. There would never be any indication of my passengers wanting to make a contribution to the petrol costs and that was a source of great annoyance to me. Even some of my work mates would want picking up but they were just the same. In those days you could get four gallons of petrol for one pound and it is easy to quote these sought of figures and think 'how cheap!'

but, at the same time, you have to look at what you were earning against what is being earned today, and for that reason you will see that there wasn't really such a difference. It was expensive even then to run a car.

One weekend, Sean and Bob wanted me to take them to a dance in Lutterworth on a Saturday night and I agreed that I would take them and I would bring them back with just one proviso. This was that I would be leaving the dance hall car park in Lutterworth at 1 am and no later. But it's amazing, even when people are having a free ride they go the whole hog and, of course, the one o'clock departure time was very quickly forgotten. But I will tell you something, they learned a lesson that night because I left Lutterworth at ten past one with no sign of them anywhere and the next day they were very unhappy, moaning and groaning about having to walk back from Lutterworth. I said the next time you go out with me when I tell you what time I am leaving you will take me seriously. I had to be in work at 7.15 am and I wasn't going to be late because two people had no sense of responsibility.

One character who played a big part in my life at about this time was Jack Chidlow who I met at Redland's Tiles. Jack was a country lad like me. He and his family had moved from Shropshire to Clifton and his family worked for a family at St Thomas Cross. However, like most things when country lads get married and have a family the care-free ways that had been experienced before would fall by the wayside. They would suddenly find that their meagre earnings from farming would be running into diffi-culties with providing a house and keeping children. In most cases, the wives of these country lads would be urging them to work in industry, not farming, to see if it could give them a better quality of life. Jack had been an outdoors boy all his life and was an extremely competent, honest person. In fact, the farmer he worked for often took him to the south of France training horses and, of course, Jack would have dearly loved his country way of life. It was the only thing he had ever had experience of and although he liked a pint he was an extremely hard working man. He was punctual too. You could set your clock by Jack's arrival time. In addition to his full-time job at Redland's he used to drive the bus collecting the workers when Redland Tiles introduced the single decker for this purpose. He was a very reliable timekeeper and would have got a bit of extra money for driving the bus, which was always useful when you had a family and a home to keep.

Jack had said to me many times that he knew I was not happy in self catering digs in Windsor Street and that if I wanted him to he would speak to Dot, his wife, about having digs with them as she used to cater for two students for the AEI – John Walsh and Kelvin who I was later to meet. It was true that I wasn't really happy with my digs at this time. Of course it was not funny when you have been at work all day to have to go back and sort your own evening meal out, and that was part of the living in digs life that I couldn't get on with. But I suppose, like everything, there is nothing perfect. Anyway, this day Jack came to me and said to go and see Dot, as they would both be in the Crow Pie pub and we would work out what I was going to do.

The Crow Pie pub had a reputation. It is alleged that many a man had his dinner laid before him on the pub table as he watched the rear end of his wife disappearing out of the door. This could happen when the attractions of the pub had overtaken the desire for their meal and time had run away with them. As they say, the wrath of a woman is worse than fire, and some of them would not take kindly to the timekeeping that some of their husbands would be happy to keep. I suppose this could be one of the reasons why I did not rush into accepting this new proposal to become the Chidlow's new lodger. In the end I took the plunge based on the fact that I was not one of those people who would have to visit a pub before they went home, so obviously this situation was a great deal easier for me than for some.

Of course, like all the unknown, it is always a decision that you are making without you really knowing whether you are doing the right thing or not as we don't have a crystal ball to gaze into in advance of these moves, but in all fairness it went really well from the outset and I was having a piping hot dinner ready for me as soon as I landed home each evening.

When I went to stay with Jack and Dot I was

training hard as the boxing matches were being planned in advance of me being ready. By way of extra training, Jack came up with this great idea that I should run to work and he would take my clobber in the bus for me to change into when I arrived. For Jack and the passengers on his bus, this was quite a bit of fun, but I might tell you that I didn't see the funny side of it. I would also have to run home at the end of the shift, and we worked from 7.15 in the morning until five in the evening. Nowadays I suppose I would be able to get a lottery-funded career in boxing so to speak and the training would become my work. But that was not the case in 1964.

On the way back from the tile factory in Clifton I would be able to get a spurt on going down the hill towards Thomas's Cross, but I would pay for that little sprint on approaching the hill heading for Clifton as the old bus would gain a lot of distance on me and claw back the advantages that I had gained. This would mean that there would be great craic on the bus, with the passengers shouting and hooraying at a worn out source of fun. It was all at my expense and, contrary to what a lot of people may have thought from the outside looking in, I was more sensitive to this ridicule than what I would let on. But, as they say, if you don't do the time you will pay later for those short cuts when it came to climbing in through the ropes of a boxing ring.

Boxing and the TA, as well as union work, would all be fizzing around me, but when I look back now I have no idea how I managed to keep all these balls in the air at one time. It just shows you the energy, enthusiasm and determination you have when you are young. To add to this I was always on the lookout for ways to earn a bit of extra money. A mate of mine, who worked at Redlands, was a skilled chippy and it amazed me why someone like him would ever have had the need to work at the tile works. It seems that fully qualified carpenters were not earning such a great wage as you might think for their skills. In actual fact, non-skilled shuttering carpenters in the building industry would have earned four times more than most of the skilled carpenters. Of course, these workers would not have been skilled men but they had the competence doing formwork for concreting and so on in the building industry. In general terms this would have been much heavier and dirtier work than a normal carpenter's everyday work.

However, to cut a long story short, as he had no car, Tom and I decided that we would go jobbing together. At the time I knew very little about odd jobs in the building trade, but I had the skills in that department, and I had the wheels, plus I wasn't frightened to have a go at most things. I had more common sense than a lot of skilled people, which would have been my contribution in this deal. We put an advertisement in the paper for odd jobs and the ones that came in varied far and wide in terms of what you might be expected to do. We even had a chap who had been sweeping his chimney and then found he couldn't get his brush down! Our main difficulty was pricing the jobs in a way that would make sense for the person having the job done and also give us a good return for our effort. Whatever we charged and whatever type of work we got, the deal was that it would be a fifty-fifty split. The telephone never stopped ringing with all types of work coming in, from gardening to putting up garages.

I remember we took a job for a doctor's

surgery in Rugby to lay a garage base. Now, at the tile works there used to be unwanted material (we called it pug) from tile making at the end of each shift and we had made arrangements for Oak's Wagons, a transport contractor next door to the tile works at Clifton, to collect all of this pug and take it to the doctor's surgery in Rugby. It was a ten-ton load collected from the tile works on Friday night and it was to be dropped off on Saturday morning. This was amazing stuff because what we used to do was pour water on it and it would come back to life again and become like wet concrete. We were all set. We had dug out the base by hand for the double garage. Tom didn't show up on the Saturday morning to do the job, but he had arranged for Carol's Dad to give us a hand and when we saw this mound of pug tipped in the gateway, we thought that whoever had come up with the idea of barrowing it from the gateway to the top of the site was most certainly mad. We were sure that even if you had twenty men that would not have been enough to achieve what we had to do. That was just one side of my plight. The other side was that I had no idea how we were going to achieve the dimensions that the doctor wanted and I just had to tell him that we would do our best but that he had better get his ruler out and do the measurements himself. Faced with all that, looking back I don't know how that garage ever came into being. But forty years later the garage is still fine, so, whatever we did, we got away with it.

Tom had given me great confidence in believing he was totally committed to this project but, unfortunately for me, I did not realise that he had not got the confidence in his own ability that was necessary for us to make a success of what we were about in the odd job world. We got plenty of jobs coming in where it would be a big patio window to be replaced, or doors to be renewed and replaced. But it just shows how you never can tell – the more these jobs came in the more depressed Tom became. Considering he was a young guy like myself and was thinking of getting married, I was full sure that this project could only get better as we went along. With the rate of work coming in I have no doubt in my mind that if I had chosen someone else to partner me in this venture that I would have gone into business very much earlier than I did.

As Tom was the quiet one, I was being used as the mouthpiece as you might say in the negotiation and selection of the jobs, and we were getting to be spoilt for choice; there were so many jobs coming in. We could easily have packed in work at Redlands, gone full time in the business and earned ten times more than we could have earned at the tile works. But destiny in these matters is never a perfect science. To my great disappointment Tom threw in the towel and I could not face carrying on. I was conscious that I did not have all the experience that was required as I had only been his helper. It would be 1988 before I came back into the building trade for real. I have no doubt in my mind that had I found someone who would have been more daring and responsible, it would not have taken twenty-one years for me to have ventured back into that industry. But that's another story, for another time.

It shows you sometimes that looking for a perfect situation isn't always the answer to making better progress in life, but some-times if you are brave enough, and have a reasonable grip on the subject you are about to become involved in, you sometimes can make a better job of it than somebody very well qualified but who hasn't got the bottle that is required to stand on his own two feet. I'm sure that had I concentrated more on going into a business project it would have been a wiser decision, but then again I went through the early part of my life and into my forties doing what I wanted to do and enjoyed every minute of it. After raising a family of four and paying off the mortgage maybe you just cannot have everything – but hey, wouldn't it be great if you could!

Some time after this, and a spell at a packing plant, Livingstone Alpack, I filled in an application form for a CKD packer at Chrysler in Baginton. Of course, I wasn't aware of it then but Chrysler had the contracts for the Humber car exports to Iran. I waited and waited and never heard a thing. In the end I gave up hope of anything coming of that and I had heard that there was work going with Rugby Excavations, a building and civil engineering company which was started by a few lads from the west of Ireland, and which they had built up into a thriving concern. I got a job with them in Yardley, just outside Birmingham, and I was picked up every morning near the Holly Bush public house in Rugby. I found myself working with a gang of ground workers on a housing estate in Yardley and as they say, the craic was good, but I couldn't see myself settling into this way of life for too long. Although I was getting better money than the basic pay at Livingstone Alpack, it wasn't great, even though I did more than the standard hours because at that time the need was to get the job finished quickly. I was driving massive dumpers. One morning I was asked to move a JCB away from the side of a house to allow a lorry load of topsoil to come in. Although I was used to machines with a front shovel, I was less familiar with a back-acter. However, I didn't have to move it very far and as I was only driving in a straight line, I had calculated that I would be able to do the move without having to do any adjustments to the back-acter, but destiny unknown always kicks in for me. It had been very wet on this bank and two of the seals of the hydraulic system on the back-acter weren't in the best of condition, so, when I moved forward on the bank, the back of the JCB slid down the bank. I looked back and saw to my horror that I had left a big black mark across the gable end of a brand new house. That was bad enough but, of course, it could have been worse, I could have demolished the whole lot! I suppose I was lucky that they didn't sack me, but I guess when they looked at the bigger picture they must have taken into account the conditions prevailing and made allowances accordingly. Also, knowing that there weren't too many volunteers for the big earthmover dumper, I survived again.

I wasn't too happy with work at this place as I had been climbing into the back of a van in the early hours of the morning, and then would have to be prepared to do whatever was going when I got there. It could be unloading an articulated lorry full of bricks or wheel-.barrowing topsoil into the gardens in a situation where you could have done with a hovercraft type of barrow to get over the obstacles that seemed to be everywhere on that building site. I was frustrated by how, it seemed to me, people in the building trade made life more difficult than it need have been by not observing a bit of logic. They didn't seem to be as planning the job prior to it being done. They always seemed to work from the outside in instead of working from the inside out. But I was to find out many years later the true cost of this incompetent method that was rife throughout the building industry when I became the employer rather than the employee.

It is funny how destiny kicks in when you are least expecting it and can change things just like turning out an electric light. When I got back home one night I had the shock of my life as there was a letter from Chrysler waiting for me. Chrysler, as you may recall, was American and used to be the old Rootes Motors and then went on to be Peugeot (the French outfit). Chrysler wanted me for an interview. I suppose I wondered if I was doing the right thing to lose half a day's work for an interview especially as I felt, after all this time, I had very little chance of being considered suitable for the job. After all, this was going into the great city of Coventry who had renowned models of engineering skills built up before and after the war which were second to none. Did I really belong among these people, I asked myself.

I had my interview with the Personnel Officer for the Knockdown kits (KD) section and, of course, a lot of people in these sort of jobs were not people with any background history to making cars but because they were ex military officers they would automatically get the job irrespective of whether they could do it or not. It was a question of the old school tie and, of course, personnel interviewing people were no different. The Personnel Officer was able to see from my records that I had worked in KD (Knockdown Kits section) at Livingstone Alpack, although very briefly. It almost certainly gave me a kick-start into KD Chrysler. At Baginton the plant was completely made up of knocked down kits, so destiny for once was on my side whereas all my life prior to this, destiny always fell on the wrong side. But when the interview was over I left without having any idea whether I would be successful or not. Incidentally, my interview took place at Baginton in the hangers that were once used by Armstrong Whitworth before being closed down in the '60s by Mr Wilson and his government of the day. Of course there was some merit in what they did but they could have made a better deal for the British taxpayers who had poured millions of pounds into the war industries prior to this happening only to see the hangars where thousands of people were working to be shut down and left with only echoes of the past. There was not a lot left when this great industry closed down in Baginton but they kept some of the lakes with all the huge Japanese fish intact. These lakes were there to provide a source of water in the event of a fire and came in very handy during my time there as you will see later. At the time of the big redundancy in those days it really was the sack without the money. Some people, I am led to believe, were uncontrollable in wailing and I have heard that a person committed suicide in one of those fire lakes.

It is funny that after you work in a factory for so many years you become attached. It becomes like your home and I most certainly can understand what it was like to lose the factory that you had worked in for years even though you would have been happily cursing the place the rest of the time, but when push came to shove it is odd that this steel framed building with its glass skylights had a tendency of hanging on to you like a bad smell. As I think about this today I wonder where things went wrong in the automotive industry when there was such an advantage over the majority of the competition in the field of making motor cars to where it is now with hardly a single car made in this great city. There is even talk now of one of the few surviving cars left, the Jaguar, ending up in

India or somewhere. Who could have believed this could happen? Who could believe that the owners of these companies, and the UK government, could be so stupid as to allow an industry which had taken so long to build up to include some of the finest models of cars in the world to be virtually lost. Massey Ferguson, the British Motor Co. and British Leyland have also all gone to be replaced by supermarkets, houses and flats. But at the time, of course, it was a great industry and I hoped to be part of it.

After the interview I went away and resumed work and normal life the following day and was very cross with myself for bothering to go to the interview as it cost me half a day's pay and double travel as I had to travel from Yardley in Birmingham to attend the interview. I knew how little I usually benefited from destiny unknown so I was always on the doubting side of life.

The days and weeks were passing without any communication from Chrysler. Every night when I got home from work I looked for anything from them but I never really believed there would be. But again you just cannot predict this life. I arrived home from work three weeks after the interview to be met by a letter saying I had got the job at Chrysler. It is difficult to explain or put into words, but this was the equivalent of a life-changing event for somebody like me. Even with Chrysler at that time paying me half the money that they were paying to their other operatives, it doubled my wages at a stroke. It even gave a provision for a small pension, which was brilliant considering that in the early 60s, during Harold Wilson's early period in government, his chancellor brought in a scheme where you paid £1 and they gave you 6d added to your pension. This wasn't a bad step for someone like me and another advantage was that I wouldn't have that trip to Birmingham every day. I would now be travelling half the distance. Yes, things had taken a turn for the better for once and just as well too because by this time I was married and expecting my second child, Mandy. This would certainly make life a bit easier for paying the mortgage and keeping the family.

With the influences from my background, and me being old fashioned, I felt that my wife, Carol, should not be doing full time work while she had young children at home. We did not believe in leaving a key under the mat, so to speak, for the children returning from school. That wasn't our way. But of course there is always a price to be paid for this type of judgement because some of the people I was working with at Chrysler would have husbands or wives working in Massey Ferguson, either at Banner Lane or just across the road from us on the other side of this big aircraft factory at Baginton. These people would be planning holidays in Spain and other such places whereas we would be heading off to Skegness to a caravan. We went loaded up with a load of blankets to keep us warm because we would take early holidays when we could, so that we could avoid the rip-off prices that came in later in the year. We enjoyed our little jaunts to Skegness but even with only one earner bringing money into the house, we always saved up enough for a holiday in Ireland as well so that I could visit Daisy and May, my foster aunts, and my foster father. Don't ask me how we did it. It must have been a miracle and also a Godsend that we didn't drink or smoke very much in those days.

Of course, after I was made shop steward and convenor at the Chrysler site for the T&G Union a lot of people would be after me to see if I could get them fixed up with a job at the plant. As this was a new venture with Chrysler and it was a situation evolving as we went along, the plant became bigger and took on more contracts for Iran, South Africa and many other countries in the world. In fact, the Iranian contract was the largest KD contract in the car industry in the world. However, it didn't always work out the way you planned in helping your mates get a job because one of the people that I did get a start for was my friend Maurice Burrells. That backfired on me to some extent because I had started boxing again and Maurice used to have spies reporting back to him if they were to find me smoking – I admit it, I would have the odd cigarette when I got the chance. I know people like Maurice will say 'excuses, excuses'. Well, OK if that's the case that is what I will have to accept. But I was always amazed – it didn't matter where I had the smoke, the speed that this news would get back to Maurice was quicker than the Whitley jet. Everyone would always take great glee when Maurice would be laying down the law that smoking and boxing didn't mix! The worst part of all of this was that I knew he was right, of course. It wasn't all bad news though. Sometimes having a friend working in the same place was good because Maurice used to pick me up along with three or four other lads so we all travelled in the one vehicle. Then it was a Godsend for Carol to be able to have my little mini to do her shopping and things as and when she liked. It got so bad with the mini and Carol; if for any reason it wasn't parked outside the window she would not be amused.

When you are boxing and getting home late at night or have been to events in Liverpool, Stoke-on-Trent, Nottingham, Leicester or Northampton to mention a few places, it would sometimes make it more difficult to get up on time and when Maurice arrived I wouldn't be ready. He would be sitting waiting in his car, almost spitting out his teeth with frustration. I would hop into the car in my bare feet with a bowl of cornflakes in my hands and hopefully we would not be late for work. We often had a very close shave and I would always be getting into hot water with Maurice for some of these antics. Other mornings I would be in such a pickle that I would end up putting odd socks on and then would have to put up with people taking the Mickey for the rest of the day. Of course, Maurice was indeed a true friend even though there were times when I could have done without him going on.

I find it strange, people are going on about floods today but they are not a new phenomenon. I remember the road being flooded as we were travelling towards Bretford one morning. This road flooded after a period of very heavy rain, in an area that is renowned for this type of problem and still is. As we hit the flooded area, we all bailed out of the car to push it through the water, which meant having to take off our socks and shoes and rolling up our trouser legs. We all waded through the water but one of our passengers, quite a young lad by the name of Mr Smith, was adamant that under no circumstances was he getting out of the car to push it. Rather than argue we did it ourselves but it was somewhat annoying that he was not prepared to put his shoulder to the wheel when it was necessary and in all our best interests. It makes you wonder how the human mind works because you are always coming across someone who is never satisfied and is not prepared to see what is reasonable and just lend a hand. But that is life I suppose, and it doesn't ever change.

Some people cannot see that they are being helped by others and are only interested in complaining, which to me doesn't make sense. Another of our regular passengers, old Dick, who was twice the age of the lad, would be well revved up about this particular flaw in Mr Smith's character, but in fairness to Dick he would tell it how he saw it and he lived to a good old age. He loved his garden and his allotment and would be able to quickly have his mind diverted to a more productive topic.

I worked at Baginton for eleven years and there was always something taking place that kept me and my mates fully occupied all those years ago and I have to say that we had the best job in the world but some had more difficulty realising this than others. Some of them wouldn't know they were born. We had the respect and understanding of the management, much more than we would have had in a bigger factory. In the summer we would have cool drinks laid on for the operators and in the winter I would have the soup urn to take around, so everybody could keep their spirits up to be able to deal with the task in hand. Because it was a big aircraft hanger you could imagine that it was always difficult to keep ourselves warm. The sliding doors to the yard were obviously a very big problem in letting the cold in, and in the summer it would be like an oven because of all the glass in the roof to give plenty of light. We used to have the glass whitewashed to give some protection but it was still baking hot in there so we had the cool drinks wheeled around. So, we were well looked after on the welfare front but of course, a lot of this welfare work was thrown in my direction. I would often be waiting to go into one meeting or another so it was less disruptive to have me take on some of these welfare tasks. One experience in this respect that I won't forget in a hurry was when I had the urn full of soup and I was trundling around the hangar handing out the hot soup to all the lads trying to keep warm as they worked. Unfortunately, there was a rut in the floor and the wheel of the trolley went down it and, yes, you have guessed it, the whole lot went flying. You have heard of waterfalls gushing down the mountains, well, this was a soup waterfall going through the factory. It was so embarrassing and my face was on fire, but it all happened so quickly you couldn't believe it. We all just stood and watched as the soup spread all around us – there was nothing we could do to stop it. Cleaning it up was not a pleasant or quick job for me and not something that I would forget in a hurry!

Chapter 11

The start of my Union career

An interesting but totally unexpected part of my life was my union career. I suppose people would be surprised that I ever became involved in such a thing because of my background and lack of knowledge of the 'ways of the world' but my natural fighting spirit and sense of justice made this something I couldn't ignore. The men I worked with could see that I was prepared to fight and many of them approached me to represent them when things went wrong in the workplace and I then found it possible to use common sense to get through the battles I had to fight.

My first involvement with unions came when I was voted in as shop steward and works convenor at the Redland Tiles factory. Of course the people before me who had done the job would normally just collect union dues and all other matters were left to the regional negotiating officers, but I could see no sense in taking on a duty to represent people if you weren't making a difference to their daily lives. Maybe my brain was finally developing and this came along at the right time for me.

The conditions at Redland Tiles in the early sixties were like taking a trip back into the early industrial revolution as, with the dust from the granulated dried sand and the colour matches for the tiles, you would have had difficulty recognising somebody a couple of feet away. When it was hot and the guys would be sweating, the dust would stick on their bodies – you would have thought you were on the stage at the Black and White Minstrel Show.

You can see why a lot of people in industry became very rich – there was one priority that didn't come into their reckoning and that was the conditions in which their workers operated on a daily basis. I have no idea how the other representatives over the years could have accepted the conditions when everyone was breathing this foul air, and taking the dust into their lungs. And these were ordinary human beings, working men. But if they had been machines being affected by dust they would have given them their own little filters and they would have had a maintenance procedure as to when that filter should be changed for maximum efficiency. But men were simply allowed to work in these conditions. I don't know why, but this issue was something that got me very wound up. Maybe it is because as I grew up, even though hungry and cold as a child, at least I had clean air to breathe. Who knows what damage all of this stuff did to people – it was never considered very important.

Another annoying piece of behaviour at that time was that big containers of leftover colour were disposed of by simply dropping them down where they were making up the banks with the broken tiles. This was an ongoing procedure. Today you would not get away with this sort of thing because all of this pollution ended up in the surrounding rivers, streams and brooks, and even at houses around the area the gardens would fill up with the different shades of colour. It is a good job some of today's environmental people were not running around then.

All of this sounds like ridiculous behaviour now but funnily enough, all the people running the factory had been to university and were well educated. Despite my complete lack of education, I was continuously telling the people responsible for this situation that what they were doing was madness. They thought I was mad, and a troublemaker, but I did not think that anybody should have the right to pollute the environment.

At Redland Tiles it wasn't long before we had a serious problem. It was in the Interlock and Broseley Ropeways where, in order to cure the tiles, the baked tiles coming through the ropeway had to pass through an acid bath, which burned the colour onto the tiles. Of course, this acid had a devastating affect on the continuous rope that ran through both ropeways, and if the ropes were not changed at the right time they became very dangerous indeed. They got particles like darning needles sticking out which penetrated the hands of the operators. The ropes were not very hygienic either, as they were oily, dirty and contained a certain amount of acid. As the Union representative at that time I asked the management if they would sort the problem out but, of course, they had decided that they would run as long as possible to get the full shilling out of these very badly worn continuous wire ropes. This meant that the operators were having their hands torn apart. There was also the added danger of the worn ropes catching on the operators' clothing and dragging them into the mechanism of the machinery. You have to remember that these were like needles sticking out, very sharp and very dirty, and when they had gone into your fingers or hands, leaving the dirt behind, the pain was horrific. There was no antiseptic available to protect and clean the wounds caused by the damaged wires and it baffled me as to why anybody would want to see people being abused in this way.

Now, not all of the people working at the tile works were union members. In fact, there would probably have been less than fifty percent who were. I suppose then, like now, these people didn't mind getting the better pay and conditions won by the unions but all too often were not prepared to pay for it. Nevertheless, I was concerned for everyone who worked there and felt very strongly that the management should do something about this obvious danger before somebody got seriously injured. As their union representative I informed the management that they had let the ropes become too worn and corroded but they ignored me. This resulted in the first all-out strike ever known at Redland's Tiles and indeed in the whole area of Rugby. I will remember the day that I called the strike until the day I die. We had decided what time we were stopping work and I was on my way across to the other site, at Stonewall, to find out what they were doing regarding the situation, as to whether they were supporting us or not. On the way out of the plant I noticed that the General Manager looked me in the eye without speaking. Probably he did not think for one moment that there would be sufficient people stop work in relation to this problem. When I looked back at the exit doors I saw the operators putting their heads out and looking both ways, up the yard and down to the gate at the road, and to my amazement every man jack of them headed for the gate in the direction of the road home! Of course, the management finally saw sense and replaced the ropes.

When I set out on putting all of this right,

without having been to university, college or even a proper school, I was amazed to find that a lot of people that I represented weren't as committed to improving conditions, nor had they seen the whole thing in the same light as I saw it. I suppose that is why they had put up with it for so many years. Also, when this industry began in the 17th and 18th centuries it would have been manufacturing at a much lower level than what they were churning out in the sixties. With the mechanised methods, with big machines gouging out earth and filling a lorry with one scoop and lots of technical advances that they had by then it would have meant that production methods had changed tremendously. It is little wonder, with this type of industry, that they wiped out a tremendous amount of wildlife in these islands and maybe the whole thing added to the health problems that are with us today.

I remember a little while after the strike, when a director of the company was introducing me to a new manager, he told the new manager that he would be well advised to listen to what I had got to say in relation to the members' welfare. Oddly enough, we never had another problem that called for downing tools. A desire to put things right for the ordinary workers and a strong sense of the injustice that was going on in industry stayed with me throughout my working life. It was obviously assumed that that large employers would be able to get away with virtually anything and, of course, Redlands was a huge international company then, and it is even bigger today. But what was going on was, to me, inhuman bullying on a commercial basis which was widespread throughout British industry at that time and long after.

Things were going at a blistering pace in my life at this time – time seemed to be flying by and I was still trying to earn a living despite my problems. A lot of my mates had heard of jobs going at Livingstone Alpack at Watford Gap, just off the M1. It had been a notorious motorway cafe and also a sawmill yard but was owned at that time by a Canadian packing company. They had contracts for packing the Bedford RL military lorries, Massey Ferguson tractors, and numerous other big deals. I was happy enough at the tile works at the time but it did start to un-nerve me that every day was passing and more and more of my mates were giving in their notice. I couldn't believe it when one of the fitters, Rupert, who was in his sixties and had been at the tile works for over twenty years, put in his notice. I thought it was starting to get serious when people like Rupert took such action. I couldn't see the sense in him taking the plunge as he didn't have long before he would be retiring. He was really comfortably off and didn't have a mortgage to worry about so I'm not sure what prompted his action but it did make me wonder whether he knew something that I didn't know.

The money that people were talking about, including bonuses etc. was four or five times the amount we could earn at the tile works, and for the younger people it certainly made sense for them to leave. In the end, for fear that I would be left on my own, I went for an interview at Livingstone Alpack and got the job. I then gave my notice in after being at the tile works for seven or eight years, and of course, that was a big decision for me. That decision wasn't taken lightly, believe me, as I had a mortgage and it wasn't long before the arrival of my first daughter, Debbie. I suppose that when you think about this sort of decision, and that old pal destiny unknown always lurking and lapping around, you may have to be very stupid, or very mad, and very brave, to take the different directions I was heading in, especially in view of the security at Redland's – although I knew that it was never much in terms of rewards. In 1969 my hours were from 0715 until 1715 five days a week and 0715 until 1400 on a Saturday, for which I was paid a total sum of £23 and with a baby on the way this was not very much at all. So I had the pressure of the lack of money where I was, a baby on the way, the mortgage to pay, a car to run and general living expenses. I suppose under these circumstances I simply did what I had to do. But giving up operating machines to go working with packing machinery, motors and lorries and so on would be a very big change. I had to be trained for the first six weeks during which I got a percentage of the bonus that was earned on the line. What wasn't made clear though to all of us new guys was that there was a 'feast or a famine' environment to contend with. In other words, there would often be more work than we could cope with one week and the next week there would be nothing. This was most certainly a shock to me because after the first week the whole house of cards collapsed and the packing virtually dried up. Instead of packing lorries in the end I was sweeping the yard for just day rate and, believe it or not, this turned out to be worse pay than what I was getting at the tile works. It is hard to believe that all those months with the big bonuses being earned that I had heard about were all but a distant dream.

While I had been there for six weeks without the bonus, some of the production lines during this period were flat out with work. It was just like a lottery. It would depend on where you landed as to what would be the final outcome. One week it would be the Bedford RL (a military vehicle) production line's turn to have a bonus and the next week or two it would be the Massey Ferguson tractors that would be flying. Anyway, on the seventh week, when I looked at my wages there was no difference in terms of the bonus that we were supposed to have got after six weeks. My natural sense of justice kicked in and I went to see the manager of the works to say that things hadn't turned out the way it was told to me, and, of course, at that time nothing phased me in the workplace. It wouldn't have mattered if I was having a meeting with the Queen. During my meeting with the manager he obviously tried to twist the situation to his own way of thinking but, put simply, what they had done was got a lot of people to pack in secure jobs based on misleading nonsense. As I have said, I have a mortgage to pay, and now a baby, Debbie, to look after, and maybe this gave me an extra boost of energy and determination to try and sort it all out. When that manager puffed his chest out and informed me that it wasn't a charity that they were running, I assured him that it was something I was not prepared to put up with. As I already had some experience of the trade union, I quickly informed the manager that I would seek the union's service in this matter. I then led an unofficial union mass meeting during a lunch break and laid out what I thought was the position to be taken in the matter. It was a T&G membership site and I was an NUB member, and some of the lads were too, but all of the T&G members changed en masse to the union that I was a member of. They immediately elected me as their representative. I arranged a meeting with the site manager and he soon changed his mind and accepted that when you had done six weeks training, wherever it might be, that you would automatically qualify for the bonus that was earned on site for that week.

But that did not end the matter. I was attached to the Bedford track for packing and some of the operatives on that track were not as enthusiastic about me being paid the full bonus from their track, and were muttering and moaning amongst themselves about the issue as they were implying that if I was paid the bonus then it would come out of their wages. I said, 'You don't know me, I would not operate under those circumstances'. At the end of the week when they got paid I went over to them and asked them to open their wage packets and check how much of their wages was paid to me. They did as I asked and had to admit that there wasn't a penny less than what they would normally have got. I then politely reminded them that the purpose of the union was to make things better for everybody and not to make it worse for them.

It was strange how, although I was a very new person at this site, I suddenly became very much respected by my fellow workmates. It was amazing the rate of change that took place in me in those few weeks to have come from one site and go to another to operate amongst 98% strangers. I amazed myself with how I could cope and so quickly become accepted among strangers. In the end every last Jack backed me on that site and they soon found out that the managers were unable to have such a lack of respect for them and would not be able to mess them around as they thought they might. The benefits of our making a stand soon became obvious. The whole scene had completely changed to where any changes that were being made, or any announcements that were to be made, were done properly and without rumours. But life is never straightforward. After getting all of this sorted out, the orders for the trucks to South Africa started to dry up. There were large numbers of us left with the prospect of months 'on the brush' with no light at the end of the tunnel as to when this would end and, of course, as I have said, my commitments were now such that I could no longer tolerate the situation or to allow myself to go backwards. I had to go forward so changes in my working life were on the cards again for me.

Chapter 12

Meeting Carol

As well as developments in my union career and in where I worked, there were still vast changes taking place in my life. I was, as always, working hard to save up for my two goals in life – to buy a car and to own my own house – and I was having some success in both these areas although progress was frustratingly slow and I know that I didn't always make the right decisions. It was around this time that I traded in my Sunbeam 250 BSA twin scooter for a brand new mini car. I bought it, a de luxe model, at Parkside Garage in Rugby for £500. I can still remember it being so new you could still smell the paint, but I missed the old scooter so much. But that, as they say, is progress. Considering the impossible childhood that I had survived, to think that I would ever have had a brand new mini was, to me, breathtaking. For other people who came through a normal life but hadn't got a silver spoon in their mouth it still would have taken a lot of effort I guess. But, although I was very pleased with myself and my new acquisition, I suppose when you look at it I would have been a lot better off financially keeping my scooter or catching the bus.

I was also part way to achieving my ultimate aim of buying my own house and, of course, normal people, as you might say, would also be excited about buying a house but when you come through what I have come through, and had the experience of being in digs, buying my own house could not happen quickly enough and it was forever on my mind. But then again, for now, that was just a dream. Most people would be thinking of getting married at this stage in their lives, not buying a house, but in my case I had not even got a girlfriend, which was adding to my problems of trying to be normal. But the house was all-important to me. When you are young, you don't always do the right thing. I was given advice by a Hungarian chap, a refugee who lived nearby, who said that I would be better buying a large house on the Lower Hillmorton Road in Rugby. He said there would be enough flats for three lads plus a pad for myself, and, of course, when you worked this out, the man was talking an awful lot of sense. But, guess what, I was having none of it and with the deposit that I paid on the car I could have brought the same house that he was on about and in five years time, with me letting the house out in flats, I would have had it paid for. This house would have cost, at that time, about £3500 but ten years later it would have been valued at over £60,000 but the mini, in contrast, had got more holes in it than a colander after ten years and I got just £50 for it! Not a good move.

I did occasionally have a girlfriend but it was never an area in which I felt confident. At this point I had not seen Violet (one of my first girlfriends who I so nearly made a commitment to) for some time and all the doubts and insecurities about whether I could ever have a normal life started coming back to me. I often wondered had I made the right decision about being wary of going to the caravan with Violet and I often asked myself whether I should have been bolder and taken the devil by the horns come what may. I was forever wondering whether this would be a decision I would regret for the rest of my life as I had had the chance to be with a wonderful girl who I loved very much and respected even more. Had I let all of this opportunity run through my hands like sand would have done at the seaside? These are the sort of questions you often ask yourself when you are young and as insecure as I was, and I wondered if there would ever be another chance for me to redeem myself, or was this the end of a perfect romance for somebody who was so ignorant of human relationships at that time.

At this time I was lodging with Jack Chidlow and his wife Dot. I felt comfortable in these lodgings and they both treated me very well. Only one problem was apparent. Jack's wife would like to have the dinner on the table before he had turned the bus engine off, and she expected nothing less than strict punctuality. But, for me, having been brought up in the Wicklow Hills there was no timetable in my head to stick to. It was very difficult to get my head around as to why people could get themselves worked up into a frenzy just because people weren't going to be back at a set time. I didn't give it a thought that this dinner could be a problem because if it had been cold I would still have eaten it. If I wanted a hot dinner I knew that I would have to make arrangements to be there on time. It seemed simple to me. Unfortunately some women have fixed ideas about the dinners being served and God himself would not have been able to make me change to that timetable.

One girlfriend I had was Heather. A girl that I had met at a dance with Smiggy in Welford was called Heather and her parents were landlords of the pub in Welford. She was a great girlfriend but because of my fear and OTT reaction to anyone drinking I had become very concerned that she was so comfortable with drinking a double Jameson's whiskey when I took her to the Shamrock Irish Club in Coventry. Now, I wasn't accustomed to buying drinks in pubs, and particularly in Irish pubs or clubs, so I was not aware that if I asked for a whiskey without stipulating that I just wanted a single I would have been served with a double in those days in an Irish pub or club. I can assure you I was very shocked with the price for a double whiskey in late 1964. It was enough for me to want to take a step backwards from the position where I had found myself to see which way was the best way forward. Those negative thoughts and decisions may not always have been in my best interest, (or, with destiny unknown, it may very well have been the right decision to take) but I was not prepared to take the chance. I had this fixed idea in my head that an orange sarsaparilla or a Lucozade was good enough for me and my girlfriend would have to get used to that idea. I was not happy going down any other road and that was that. Apart from my very real fear of being addicted to drink I was alarmed at the amount of money you could get through, and particularly when they smoked as well. Buying cigarettes and whiskies was not my idea of entertainment. This may seem a little mean and funnily though, all these years later, some of my grandchildren, aged between three and 15, tell me that I am very tight. However, I am not as tight as they think because my good lady wife has my money and leaves me very little after she spends it on them!

But back to Heather. Although her drinking habits sounded alarm bells for me, I know that she was probably acting just as a normal young lady would be – just wanting a bit of fun. Had it not been for all of the baggage I was carrying from my past experiences, I might have realised this at the time instead of many years later. At the time I was busy trying to present myself as being normal while fighting all these internal battles. So, as far as poor Heather was concerned, I decided that I needed time out of the situation but I must say that any guy would have considered himself extremely lucky to be able to say that she was his girl-friend. Over the dark periods of my youth and early manhood years I could only have dreamt of finding someone like her. So we left the situation where it was, as they say.

At about this time, my landlady, Dot, the matchmaker, was always on about me meeting a girl with long dark hair who would pass by the house looking like someone from another planet – a girl of dreams. When Dot pointed her out to me I had to pinch myself to think that there was a possibility of me going out with her. Anyway, I took the plunge and accepted the blind date that had been planned for some time and true to her word Dot arranged for me to meet Carol. I went and picked Carol up and took her to Clay Coton, the village where my very good friends, the Boltons lived. After this, we pro-ceeded to the Fox & Hounds pub for a game of skittles and to have the craic as they call it. What was to unfold on that night I could not possibly ever have imagined.

You will recall that some time previously I had broken up with another girlfriend, Violet. Well, she arrived that night at the Fox & Hounds with some of her friends from Coventry to meet up with friends in the village! She informed me that she was going on holiday and would be away for something like two or three weeks and that when she came back she would like me to go out with her again. She said she was prepared to be guided more by what I wanted rather than what her mother would have been insisting on. Of course, this put me in an extremely difficult dilemma. There I was, out with Carol on a blind date with my usual insecurities tormenting me. I had no idea whether this date would ever be repeated. But, of course, because of my experiences in my earlier life, I always felt more comfortable with a safety net in place. Don't get me wrong, this was not for any devious or disreputable reasons but just for my own assurance that I wasn't getting into something I couldn't get out of should I decide that was what I wanted to do. So, I was not deliberately setting out to two-time anyone but I wanted to make sure that whichever one of the three beautiful girls I was going to settle with was the right choice for me. If I was guilty of anything, it was perhaps being selfish and looking after my own interests. So this situation, which I would have to admit was like heaven, wasn't without difficulties. As they say, a drowning man will grasp at any straw and my instincts for self-preservation kicked in and I made a decision in the cold light of day that was in my interest and my interest only. There I was, a lad who really didn't expect to have one decent girlfriend, but had now got three English Roses that any man would feel so very proud to have in his garden. At the end of that eventful night at Clay Coton, I said to Violet that we would see what happened when she got back, but I think she had realised by my tone of voice, without me realising it, that there would be no further involvement and at the end of the night we went our separate ways. I chose Carol.

The next time I went for Carol I was going to take her to the Shamrock Irish Club in Coventry. I went to pick her up her as we had previously arranged but I have since found out that Carol had told her mother that if Derek came to the door to tell him she was out! Anyway, I did knock at the door and her mother, God bless her, shouted to Carol that Derek is here. There are times when you are not fully aware of all the background that starts kicking in, but destiny unknown can affect you at any time in your life, and more often than not does so without you having a clue. I know now – although I had no idea then, of course – that if it hadn't been for Carol's mother the relationship between Carol and me would have been very short lived. Although we had arranged a date after the first night we met and I turned up as planned in my nice little blue mini to take a trip to Coventry, Carol was trying to avoid me! I was only to find this out thirty odd years later. But I suppose at that time Carol hadn't worked out that maybe her mother wanted her to be with someone and wanted her to start making her own life. Carol was not amused to find herself face to face with me on her mother's doorstep. For all of my hopes that from the first time I set eyes on her she was going to be my wife, it most certainly was a very fine line between my hopes and dreams and it all actually happening.

Before we go on, let's explain what happened with the unfinished business of Heather and Violet. I was at the tile works when I had a message from one of my friends who lived in the village of Welford to say Heather wanted to know what was happening. The fog had started to clear a little bit in my mind and I sent a message back that I could not see it working with us. I would probably have placed the blame on her, when in fairness it would have been more me to blame than her because of the baggage that I was carrying. So, one down and one more to go. Funnily enough, if Violet had approached me a week or even a day earlier it could have made a huge difference, but it was just too late. Having met Carol, I felt I was now in a relationship, even though very briefly. Although Carol was seven years younger than me, I always felt from that first evening onwards that my destiny was sealed and that I would marry Carol and live with her for ever and a day. I made that decision instinctively. I never had any doubts whatsoever that she would be my wife, and when you stop and think about it there is nothing in this world that could have given me any indication as to how that happened, but believe me your destiny is often sealed without you ever having any input into it.

But even though things were looking up for me, dark clouds are never that far away. Some landladies take a very dim view of having a lodger about the house in the daytime but as I had just had my tonsils out I was going to be housebound for a few days before I returned to work as the tile works was an extremely dusty place and not a good place to be in just after an operation of that sort. I was always very sensitive to feelings of being unwanted so this made me start to make arrangements to move on. I had heard of a lady, Mrs Marshall, in Meadow Road, Newbold. She turned out to be a brilliant lady who called a spade a spade, and you knew exactly where you were with her. She made it very clear that if she said the dinner was served at one o'clock at the weekend then that would be the time it was served and if I wasn't around the dinner would be put back in the oven and however that dinner came out of the oven was the way I would get it, but that there could be no blame placed on her regarding its quality. Of course, for somebody like me who wasn't very good with the clock because of how I grew up, this was perfect for me. So there I was, on the move again.

It didn't seem five minutes since I had moved into the Chidlow's, and I suppose to be fair, old Dot did treat me like family. But their family was nothing like my family so I found it all too hard to take. Some families are gentler with how they harangue people than others are and with Dot you could not argue. She would give her all to you and then break you up. If you had been her son out playing in the garden and then run across the best carpet with dirty boots you would have been treated just the same. I suppose that was another part of family life that I had no experience of and therefore would not have understood what was happening.

Life was fine in my new digs. Although I had moved I could still see my old friends and I would occasionally see the Boltons at Clay Coton, for whom I had a very special fondness. I was also still involved with the Trades Union movement at work as Shop Steward for the GMW Union. Who could have believed that someone who had so little confidence (and what little I did have had been regularly knocked out of me before I was nine) could have built a life so full. In the five years that I had been in England how fast my brain must have grown from the strangulated boy I had been prior to leaving Ireland. I had also had my boxing bouts with the Willenhall Amateur Boxing Club and had driven all over the place. I have even taken a friend, Dave Olner, to the Liverpool Stadium. This is the sort of place that I could only have dreamed about all those years ago.

Carol and I had been going out for a good while and we had built up quite a nice social life. We went many times to the Bamba Club in Foleshill Road, Coventry, and often would have gone to the Holbrooks Field where they used to play Gaelic games and hurling. One weekend, The Bachelors were performing live nearby and it was no surprise to me that Carol wanted to go to see them. Not only did she want to see them sing but she also insisted on being right next to them to try to get an autograph. Unfortunately it turned out to be a very bad situation for us because we went early and found ourselves at the front of the queue and everybody was pushing and shoving from the back of the hall. This continued for a while, with us feeling badly jostled but with Carol still determined to get the autograph, until the crowd behind us were pushing to such an extent that the security staff moved and we thought we were going to be crushed to death. This was really scary and I know it taught me a lesson not to stand at the front of a crowd ever again. But I am very pleased to say that we did indeed manage to get the Bachelors' autograph.

Having been living in England for a few years I came to realise that going away on holiday seemed to be the thing that matters more than anything else. It seemed to me that people would have to have one or two weeks away, irrespective of whether they had the money or not. For somebody like me who worked 24/7 and had never had a holiday in his life, I found this pretty surprising. Carol's mother and father told me they were going to Southsea that year and I was invited to join them there. They told me what time they were going and informed me that I was not to be late under any circumstances. My God, weren't they pushing it knowing my record with regard to timekeeping! Most of the others went by coach – Carol's two sisters and her parents, while her brother went down on his motorbike. In those days boyfriends would not have been asked to stay in the same house as their girlfriends or her parents. I would have to find a different place to stay but, as always, I would be very careful when spending money with some 'seaside shark' that only wanted to make money out of me. I wasn't risking that so I had decided that I would borrow a tent.

Although I had changed an unbelievable amount and in many ways since I had arrived in England, I was not totally in the English way of thinking. I assumed things like this would be the same as when I was in Ireland and that you could put a tent up anywhere you could find a bit of space and not give it a second thought. So, I just pitched my tent fairly near where Carol was staying and I asked no questions – I just got on with it. But I was in England where there are rules and regulations. There were loads of other tents and caravans there as well but luckily everybody was so busy so no-one came around to hassle me as to what I was doing there. Even so, things did not go completely smoothly with me and my tent. We had a few storms and one day when I went back, I found my tent flattened. I often woke up in the night to see the stars in the sky.

The digs that Carol and her family were staying in could have accommodated a dozen people or more. The rooms were large, but that made no difference, it was out of bounds to me. One morning Carol got her brother to bring her out to meet me, as really she wanted to be on holiday with me without her parents – you know what girls are like. But things were not going to go completely right for her either on this holiday. They trundled on to the camp site on her brother's 90cc Honda, but because of the wet grass and the rough terrain, it tipped them off. As they fell off the bike it landed on poor Carol's leg and gave her a nasty burn. Despite these problems, I have to say I loved every minute of that holiday.

With Southsea and Southampton being close there was so much to do and so many places to visit. I couldn't believe how great a holiday could be. Up to going away with Carol and her family I had never been able to see the point of them! We visited HMS Victory and wandered all around it and, me being a dreamer, I drifted back centuries in my mind and was able to visualise that period of history in its full glory. I imagined rushing around under attack from the Spanish Armada and bumping my head on the low ceilings. And imagining the pirates' stories that the sailors would have gathered in their lifetime's travels took my imagination into overdrive, whilst I stood on the deck of HMS Victory. Carol and her family all thought I was mad. But I felt some magic spell had been cast upon me. As they say in Ireland, I was gone with the fairies.

Visiting Southampton and seeing all the great ships in the harbour, with their plumage exposed for all to see, left you in no doubt that Britannia ruled the waves and I was impressed by all of the history that would have surrounded the seafarers. What an impression that would make on any young lad who might have had an idea of wanting to join the Royal Navy. I could only look on the scene with amazing pride. To go and see that great passenger liner the Queen Elizabeth, which was probably on one of its last visits back to the UK after crossing the

Atlantic Ocean from America, was a fantastic experience. I had always loved ships and the history of shipping, and up to that time had only ever seen photographs, or television programmes, of the great liners but to actually be able to see this magnificent liner was an amazing experience for me.

As I look back now over all the years I am extremely shocked and saddened to think all of this has now gone. There is no question that these islands were truly great in every sense of the word then, but my fear today is that with some of the political decisions taken, and with us exporting work out of the country whilst keeping millions of people in all corners of the world, if someone doesn't wake up to this very soon these great islands will become no more than a banana state. Never mind, I am off again; let's stick to the job in hand.

We were lucky enough to have had a brilliant spell of weather for our holiday and wherever you went the flowers that were in bloom were a picture. The big parks were all perfectly tended and set out for the public to enjoy. There is no question that when you get good weather in the British Isles and Ireland there is nowhere better. Of course, during that time Britain was still in the twilight of exploring and developing and so the hovercraft was running from Southsea over to the Isle of Wight. Again, for someone who had only heard about this and had just seen pictures of it I never paid that much attention to the hovercraft. As we were wandering around we noticed that there was a sign advertising trips to the Isle of Wight and thought maybe it would be nice to take a trip. The fee was ten shillings per head one way. We thought, OK it's a lot of money but it's a trip of a lifetime if you have never done it. So, we found out that the price on the railway ship for the return journey was a few pennies cheaper per head and decided we would only go one way on the hovercraft and book on the railway ship for the return journey. Whilst we were taking off and landing, the stones and gravel that were being picked up under the skirt of the hovercraft was something to see. It was a wonderful trip and a great experience, and at least we can say we know what it was like to travel on the early prototype hovercraft of 1966. I suppose you could say it was as good as a trip to the moon as to me it seemed just as far away from being normal.

We were so busy going to all the different places that there had not been time to see the television or to hear the news for a while and I had made a very serious error of judgement in not realising before the holiday that in actual fact we were away at the same time as the 1966 World Cup. I got a strange feeling that whenever I happened to wander any-where near a shop window with televisions I was being shepherded away and wasn't being encouraged to stay a minute longer in that vicinity than necessary. Towards the end of the holiday it suddenly dawned on me that the World Cup was being played out and it was looking likely that England was going to be in the final. I was, of course, desperate to watch this match, but Carol had her own agenda all worked out with her family so that the World Cup could be played with the greatest of ease without me having to be bothered with it. However, on the Friday I happened to be talking to some people who told me England were in the final the next day. I immediately made plans to get back home as quickly as possible. I told Carol that we would head back early to miss the traffic, but on the way down she had noticed a quaint little café and she said she would like to call there on the way back. Needless to say, at that time nobody had said anything about the World Cup.

I continued to plan. I knew that on this trip stopping at that café was totally out of the question in terms of time. In those days I was not a wild, mad driver. I would usually go with the flow, but Carol couldn't work out why I seemed to be going faster than I would normally drive. In answer to her murmurings, I just said I was trying to get back before the build up of traffic. So when we came to this lovely little café I have to say I pretended I hadn't seen it until it was too late and I was a mile or two up the road before the penny had dropped. At that point Carol had no idea as to why I wasn't being more flexible to her needs. She thought that I had just drifted along but I didn't get off scot-free even on this small point. She concentrated her conversation for the better part of the return trip back on the fact that I hadn't stopped at the perishing café. As a compromise, I stopped at a café that wasn't so flash or so picturesque; one that you wouldn't want to stop in a minute longer than was necessary. It was a lay-by hot and cold batch bar where we stopped for refreshments, to Carol's horror. If looks could have killed I would be dead. I rushed the rest of the journey and flew off to my new digs in Meadow Road, Newbold, where Carol and I were able to watch the last ten minutes of that fantastic World Cup match. The things we do to be able to see a bit of football! To most females it would never have crossed their minds that they might be missing something by not watching one of the great events in British history. I took some stick over that episode long after the effects of England winning the World Cup had worn off.

In the few months before our holiday I had changed beyond all recognition. I was boxing and also setting up the Newbold club. I had started to walk tall where before it must have been difficult to even see me in terms of my character. Everything was going right for me for a change. I had found a most wonderful person to share my life with. Now I had to prepare the stage for the next chapter that was to unfold in my life; I had to grow up very quickly. I had to put aside dreaming and begin to bite the bullet as now it was getting very serious with Carol and she was to become my wife very soon. I don't know why, but I had made up my mind that without any doubt we were going to get married, and I don't know how to explain the situation because I never asked her would she marry me or did she want to spend the rest of her life with me. I don't know if I was very naïve but whatever it was, no doubts ever dawned on me.

But, as they say, all good things come to an end and with the holiday – and the World Cup – over, it was back to work. At 7.15 on Monday morning I was back at Redland Tile and into the real world. Carol was the same, she had to be ready for work at the Portland Cement offices in Rugby, but in her mind there was only one thing she was concentrating on and that was the plans for her big step in life which was to get married. Girls are different, if I may say this, in that there would be no other interfering matters in their lives other than the plans for the wedding, whereas for me it was just an extra task to deal with. I would still have to fill the hoppers with sand at the tile works, be involved with the GMB union as I was their representative, and of course there was still the boxing as well as the TA – they were all part of the mix.

Carol changed my life. I could never have known how important it would be to my life when I was introduced to her all those years ago by Dot Chidlow. I could never have guessed at how things would turn out. Prior to that time I was in an uneasy period of my life. I didn't think I would ever meet a girl who would be so loving, caring and understanding as Carol turned out to be. It really was like winning the lottery. I can still see her coming through the Fareham High School as a short cut from work, with her dark hair and soft loving eyes – she surely was just a peach. It all seems to have fallen into place from that one intervention by poor old Dot Chidlow, who now has sadly passed on. Who could have imagined that 42 years later that little scheme of Dot's is still running its course – we now have four daughters and nine grandchildren, the products of an adventure that was, in part, just a little bit of mischief and teasing. Who would have believed it would turn into a permanent fixture? I bet Dot never imagined that her little bit of matchmaking would last all these years. Dot loved matchmaking and always continued to keep an eye out for a likely girl for me. I suppose that is where destiny unknown kicks in because some of the other girls that were in the frame for Dot's matchmaking antics were, from the point of view of an outsider looking in, very likely candidates and they might have thought that I shouldn't ignore the possibilities. But I was having none of it. I just knew that Carol was the one for me. But life has its own twists and turns and none of us can imagine how it is all going to end up.

When I met Carol it meant that I was no longer going out unaccompanied with my mates as Carol became part of the team, so to speak. This meant that when we went to the pubs, the old Shamrock Club in Cox Street, Coventry, Wicksteed Park, Stamford Hall or Twycross Zoo, she always came along. We used to like to go to Stamford Hall, near Clay Coton, as it was very countrified and spacious and a very pleasant place to be in, with the lakes and rivers nearby. During this period my foster brother Sean and his girlfriend would sometimes be part of the party.

I had had a dream for years that I would buy

a home of my own and I decided now that I must go and have a look at houses and find a way of buying one. Of course I had no idea of anything about this whole house buying business and about mortgages and deposits. All of that was foreign to me and I had no one that I could turn to that I knew had experience in these fields. Normally you have parents, or people that have bought houses in the past, that can guide you in making the right decision but I was not in that position so I ended up talking to an estate agent about buying a property. When I look back it seems there was no mountain too high to climb and when you consider that I was a person that had been so down-trodden for so long I wonder where did I get the confidence and wisdom, as well as the understanding, to make these momentous steps that I was setting out to take.

I had a look around several properties and decided that 85 Fareham Avenue was where the wheel of fortune was going to stop. This was even before Carol had any idea and even before I had proposed to her. In actual fact I had bought 85 Fareham Avenue a year before I got married on the 25th March 1967 and you would have thought that maybe I would have been in a mood to impress my beautiful new flower by being a little bit boastful about the big decision that I had made that I was wanting her to share in. But I suppose it all happened so quickly. There was so much going off. I was involved in so many different things that I didn't have time to try and be boastful and make an impression. Keeping all the balls in the air was enough for me to cope with. When you think about some kid coming through what I had been through, and, because of my lack of education, always having to take low paid jobs, you might be forgiven for wondering how on earth I had managed it all. I had achieved my ultimate goal – I had bought a brand new mini and now here I was buying my own house. One reason, I guess, that a lot of people in my position might not have managed to achieve this would be that too many young men spent a long time looking into empty glasses and not enough time into realising that the more empty glasses were around them the less chance they would have of achieving anything or being able to be anything, and would always end up needing digs or rented properties. I just have to be grateful that the strands that ran through my logic overcame all of the likely temptations that were there to trap me. It would have been so easy to turn down that lane, the comfort zone, the illusion zone, the no hope and no end zone.

Of course, I eventually did take her to see the house and when Carol, my then fiancée, was surveying her new territory it was a wonderful picture. The sight of her smile, her wonderment and appreciation of being in her own home I can remember still. She was still a very young girl and, of course, all of her dreams and hopes were being realised as she surveyed each and every nook and cranny of the property. As quick as a flash of lightening she was deciding what she was going to be doing in this room and how she would want things set out in that room as she wandered around the house. I have no doubt in my own mind that she didn't think it was a good idea to fully inform me of all of her desires and requirements. Girls don't. They like to have a time bomb or two left dotted about to keep the male on their toes, as you might say.

Straight after the excitement of looking at the house that was to become our first home together, we had to leave everything on hold, as I had then to head off to a TA camp near the Brecon Beacons for two weeks. That suddenly changed the temperature. How Carol hated those fortnights. It was a good job I never got called up to do a full tour of duty as she used to go into a mood for a couple of weeks before I went to a two week TA camp and spend the week after I came back saying how sorry she was for being so silly. Of course. in those days that bit of extra money that I got from the TA made a lot of difference and we ended up getting one or two things and being able to do a few things that we would not have been able to do had I not made that sacrifice. In those days the TA would have family days to try to break down barriers and to bring the wives and girlfriends into what would have been considered to be part of the family. There would be days when we would go to Six Hills and have the women driving lorries and Land Rovers whilst the husbands and boyfriends were in competition shooting plates at the Six Hills rifle range. I wonder how many of the young ladies and wives from all of those years ago can still remember their near misses in the lorries as the men would be running for their lives to avoid them whilst they were doing their manoeuvres on a hot day on those days out. Some of the wives and girlfriends had a great weekend but that did not stretch to compensating for me being away for a fortnight as far as Carol was concerned. There was no substitute, and no bribe that I could find that would ensure that she simply accepted that I was going to be away every now and again.

But the time that we were courting we certainly lived to the full. We never wasted a minute. We covered thousands of miles and made countless new friends. It most certainly was an enormous transformation in my life. Carol helped me such a lot – and still does – especially with the one area that I found so difficult. If I needed a letter doing, or some awful form to fill in, yes, you have guessed it, Carol got the job. I suppose to some degree I allowed myself to wallow in my comfort zone in getting Carol's help to do all this work when maybe I should have persevered a bit more myself but it is often easy to look back and maybe see that we could have done things differently. There is no doubt that my relationship with Carol is one area of my life that I can look back on and think of as the great success story it was, and still is, which started with that lovely sixteen year old girl that I met all those years ago. The enormity of my success in this area was brought home to me very forcefully when our daughters organised a 40th wedding anniversary party for us on the 25th March 2007. Sometimes you are apt to take so much for granted with life flying past you, that when some of your children make statements at such an event as our party you have to stop to digest them properly – they take the wind out of you. I suppose you spend your time worrying about how things were not perfect and how you could have done things differently through the years and you forget what their thoughts might be. So, what were their thoughts and experiences growing up with a family on the English side and their father who was an unwanted child? There is no doubt that kids from our sort of relationship are going to be somewhat lopsided in terms of their relations from my side of the family, i.e. grandparents, uncles and aunts that they never knew. It is perhaps a good job we were too busy when they were growing up to worry about all of this. The point I am getting to is that when my daughter Mandy, who grew up in our little two bed-roomed bungalow in Southey Road, Rugby, which we had converted with a loft conversion to give us an extra bedroom for her, quite calmly and very lovingly made a statement, read from her notes, that their experience was that of growing up in a 'house of laughter'. Now, I didn't take this in on the night as it came out quite casually – but very sincerely. It was only afterwards that it was like the after effects of an earthquake and I was completely bowled over by such a simple statement. I don't think that any kids could have better memories of their childhood than to remember being in such an environment as that. There was nothing very scientific or poetic in the flow of these words as they came from my daughter but I have to say that they sucked the air out of my lungs with total shock and pride. To think that we raised our four girls in a modest little home, and they can remember their lives growing up in that environment all to do with laughter! I don't know, but I think that speaks volumes, but again I have to leave it to others to formulate their own views. I don't have any doubt in my mind that I could not think of such a simple, straightforward few words that would have such an impact. So I suppose when people see that somebody who has come through their childhood in the circumstances such as I was exposed to, that their offspring can only have memories of happiness, then that is truly a success story that I am proud to tell. I may not have conquered the interest or ability to have offshore bank accounts and money always being a problem, but I know if I was faced with that sort of choice I would always want to accept the house of laughter against wealth.

Of course, I can't take all the credit. When my girls were going to school Carol was a full time mother, unlike what is only too common today and which can in no way be separated from the mayhem, disrespectfulness and uncontrollable tearaways that seem to be everywhere, with kids running wild and having no idea what is right and what is wrong. Most of these unfortunate children do not know what it is like to have the attention of a full time mother. We all pay a very high price for this. I think we must take bringing children up properly far more seriously than we are currently doing. We now have areas in the UK where uncontrollable children are not just wrecking their own lives but also the lives of other people in their neighbourhood. We have now most certainly got ourselves into a terrible phase where gangs of young people have got nothing better to do with their lives than to mock and knock seven bells out of innocent people. This cannot go on and I pity any parent today raising children in this society where they can do as they wish without any accountability. This cannot be right.

Anyway, back to those pre-wedding days in the 1960s. The big day was looming and we were striving to get bits and pieces for our 'bottom drawer'. Life must be a lot easier for people who have got families on both sides who can contribute to giving a young couple a kick start in their life. It is always going to be difficult when one side of the relationship has no family members to contribute to the young couple's future together. I think this is the sort of little thing that you don't even think of, as you go through life, doing your best. But have no illusions, the repercussion of these gaps and voids will always crop up and will never go away. There will always be occasions when you miss the contribution, whether financial or just the moral support that a family can give, and also one side of your family is going to be missing for your kids and grand-children. So, looking at this from another point of view, what must it be like for people such as my mother and her family to know that her son, grandson or nephew would never be able to get any help from his side of his family?

I have to say I was lucky that I had some good friends who helped out with bits and pieces and that my landlady in Newbold, Mrs Marshall in Meadow Road, gave me the double bed that I had in digs, a ward-robe and a few other things to help out. She was such a kind person and never interfered in anybody's life other than to try and be helpful. She was not a rich person, just a normal, run-of-the-mill lady, but her concerns were obviously to assist a young couple starting out in life who really didn't have very much at all. Our friends also contributed bits and pieces on our wedding day and that made such a big difference in our lives from that point onwards.

There were a few times when I was expected to sort out the banns to be read in church, but the vicar couldn't fit the wedding into the church calendar and I had to go back repeatedly until I got what I wanted. This worried me as I continually fussed about what others thought. I knew that Carol's parents would not be amused when I was telling them that the banns had not been read yet. I felt uneasy about this but it was totally out of my control, and it was only the vicar who could deal with this matter. Even so, I felt so guilty that maybe I hadn't made the vicar take seriously enough what I was saying. I suppose, in the background, all these sort of moves were being noticed and taken a lot more seriously than I realised – probably with good reason, as it may well have appeared to onlookers that I was not putting my weight behind the efforts to arrange the wedding. And of course, you can be assured that a young bride would be taking these matters extremely seriously and there would be nothing else on the planet that would have been comparable to her wedding plans.

All the problems with the wedding arrangements were eventually overcome and, with the help of all the friends and Carol's relations, and my landlady, we were also having success in getting the house ready to live in. After doing quite a bit of remedial work the house was ready to live in. Getting the bed and wardrobe moved in was down to me. So, I can claim that I did the removal into our first house – our removal van was in fact my mini car. The furniture was loaded on the rack on top of the mini and off we went. Of course, we didn't have spare funds to do the job properly so I would have to say I was pleased with my accomplishment. There was no problem to me that was insurmountable and not conforming to order would be the norm. They will have to put on my tombstone 'He did it his way'.

I did all this moving, decorating and planning well before the wedding but I would not be living in the house for another twelve months. I learned that my foster brother, Sean, was now living in a caravan, and a leaking one at that, with a new baby. Although I could never understand his lack of planning for the future, I felt I had to help him out yet again. As I had got 85 Fareham Avenue not far off being fully furnished and, knowing my foster brother's plight, I suggested to him that he would be welcome to move in there and save up for a down payment on a place of his own. He would, of course, move out after Carol and I got married. But things never turn out the way you plan. He lived there for twelve months without paying any gas, electric, or rates (as it was then), but when we came to move in, to Carol's horror, they had done nothing whatever about getting their own place.

But that revelation was still to come. First we had the wedding. The big day came when we got married at St Mark's Church at Bilton near Rugby and had our little reception in the Community Hall in Hillmorton. They say sometimes dreams can come true and in this case I have to confess that mine certainly did. When I look back to when I was sitting in the pew in the church with all of the doubts and misgivings which hit you for a few seconds, I now know that there was never any need for any such doubts. But of course from where I had come this was one enormous step to take. You have to understand that I was old fashioned in my thinking. As far as honour was concerned, a husband's duty to look after a wife and family would have been something that would not have been negotiable. I knew that I would have to deal with whatever was to confront me in the years to come, even with the unknown of a family that had still to come. The whole thing seemed so daunting to me as I sat in that pew but, nevertheless, I knew that Carol was the one for me. But there I was making a commitment that no matter what I did I was going to make sure I carried out my duties and my responsibilities and if that meant that I wouldn't have money to spend in other areas, just too bad. I suppose that is one reason why we managed to get to celebrate 40 years of marriage. I think there are too many young people today who have got it in their heads that if it's a choice between carrying out their responsibilities to their families and visiting the pub, or a night club, or even, today, a casino, the family would have to take a place at the back of the queue.

Of course, as she entered the church Carol would have seen how out of balance the number of relations were. My side of the church was somewhat depleted, to say the least, as there was only my foster brother, the nearest thing to any relation being there on my part, and the rest of it was made up with friends. The good friends who were there for me covered up my lack of relatives – and my embarrassment. Our reception later at the Community Hall was just what we wanted. Everyone who came to the wedding had a great time, it was good craic and they even played a few bits of Irish music for my benefit. A day to remember to be sure.

Chapter 13

The honeymoon and after

After our wedding reception Carol and I were taken back to Fareham Avenue. We didn't head directly for our honeymoon destination – Muswell Hill in London – because I had made arrangements to go to Coventry on the Sunday to see a hurling match which was organised by the Coventry Irish connections. St Finbarr's were having a special team over from Ireland to play their club team at their field in Holbrooks. I thoroughly enjoyed what in those days the Irish called 'the clash of the ash'. I think Carol was somewhat mystified as to why we hadn't headed straight for London on the Saturday, but I really couldn't see the point of missing such a match when we could simply delay the honeymoon by a day. But never mind, Carol forgave me and after the match we went straight to London. I hadn't given the journey, or the route of my journey, a second thought. It is funny, when you are young there is nothing that is too complicated for you to overcome and without any instructions, or even a map, we ended up at the hotel in Muswell Hill, where we spent the rest of our honeymoon. We went to Parliament Square, St Paul's Cathedral, Westminster Abbey, Buckingham Palace, Kensington Palace, and we watched the changing of the guards. We had a great time taking in all those wonderful sights and the London culture. The demonstrations and parades taking place against various issues just passed us by. Yet there were people coming off buses and trains and taking up their campaigns as if the very existence of life on earth depended on their enthusiastic input. They were so intent on their desire to change whatever the issue may have been which had aroused them to such an extent that they felt they had to explode upon London that they seemed to think that everybody there was going to be taking notice of what they desired. But isn't it funny, when it comes down to it, ninety-nine percent of the Londoners – and visitors like us – would not have known anything about the protest, nor could they care less.

Carol certainly enjoyed going around all the

wonderful places and going to Buckingham Palace was very special for her, but, of course, I was simply overawed by all of it. We had a brilliant week. At the hotel where we were staying a fellow guest was a Spanish boxer. He was in London to box one of the big names in the UK, but I was under instructions from my new wife not to get involved with him and I had to come away from London without knowing any more about him. In the setting of all of the wonderful sights of London my imagination once again came to life. I am one of those people who can actually switch on as I am viewing the sights and turn the clock back to whatever period I need to be in and can imagine all of the events that would have taken place in historic places such as the Houses of Parliament and Buckingham Palace. In the Tower of London, where the great and not so great came to a sticky end, my imagination was especially busy.

Of course, honeymoons do not last forever and we arrived home safe and sound. Quite how we managed to get down to London and back in one piece I will never know, as some of those London drivers were driving as if they had a sixth sense and were somehow or other protected from being demolished by a greater force than themselves. Of course, it was all part of the way they lived and you could only take your hat off to them, but I am glad that I don't have to live at that speed. Back at Fareham Avenue and life carried on without any let up. I was still rushing to boxing, the TA and work, and now we had the added problem that our lodgers had become more permanent than we had intended.

I was amazed at how Sean and his wife had made themselves so comfortable in our house. For example, when I was rushing out to work in the mornings and would have everything judged to the second, Sean's wife would come down and empty the kettle that I had just boiled, and proceed to make the baby's bottle. This lack of thought will always shock me. I was rushing to work. Why would she want to do that when she could have waited ten minutes until I was ready and then there would not have been any problem. The sheer lack of consideration for someone who was, in fact, helping them so much was shocking. People say that there is not room for two women in one kitchen and that was certainly the case at

Fareham Avenue on more than one occasion, but in this case it was not two women but one woman and one man. I found that I frequently had to fall out to get my point over. Then I would feel sorry that I had said anything when she started crying! Of course there was worse than these little niggles to come, because money would often rear its ugly head. My foster brother had taken on work where he wasn't paid a fixed amount on a regular basis. He was in sales and what money he earned was determined by what sales he made. What I didn't know at the time was that he was living the life of Riley, and making sales or not making sales was not that important to him as he knew that all his bills were being paid by Carol and me. Understandably, Carol often used to be in moods about the situation, but I didn't really understand this because she would not tell me the whole story until much later. Things were going on that I sometimes didn't know about. For instance, Sean's wife was adding her shopping list onto Carol's list because Sean was not giving her any money and Carol was getting very frustrated by it all. She was thinking here am I, just married and going out to work and I have already got someone else's child and its parents to keep. In the end of course I had to say to Sean in no uncertain terms that this situation could not go on any longer and in the end we managed to get them out. This was a great relief to Carol and I hadn't realised just how uptight she was with all this business going on. It was certainly not a good position to be in when you had just got married.

So, even though I was a married man I was yet again suffering problems with my foster family and I was still trying to sort out their lives as well as my own. Yes, I was a fool. He never had to pay a penny for rent, rates, gas or electricity, as I picked up all of those bills for him. I have come to the conclusion that there can be no justice. There are no rewards for people trying to do the right thing by sorting out the ones who continually had no respect or moral judgements, or sense of pride in achieving their own targets without having to devour someone else's hard earned pay. But then again, that should not have been a surprise to me because the signs were certainly well lit up. I should have known that there was only one way that Sean was prepared to go and that was to take all he could as long as he could get away with it. I still don't know how someone you knew and grew up with could be like this and, I think I was, at this stage, pretending and kidding myself that this was not really happening.

It must have been very difficult for Carol to observe what was going on and she would know that there would never be any end to it. She could see what I didn't seem able to see – that the more he got the more he would want. She must have felt that my softness and naïvety would have its own downside in the fullness of time. But again, you plough on. You have to cope with the situation as it is and pray to God that you are rescued somehow so that you can put your feet down on a firm place. I suppose it is easy to say that I was soft and naïve but, after saying that, humanity must kick in and to see a newborn baby having to live in a leaking caravan in a country where, you have to agree, we get our fair share of rain, is not good. Surely no-one with a heart would be able to let that carry on. I was thinking of Sean's new wife as well, but you can be assured that she never thought of me, and even today the pair of them would have as much interest in offering me a drink as in flying to the moon. It is still hard for me to get my head around why have I ended up being with a family who were as dysfunctional as the one I ended up with.

Luckily Carol and I were able to recover from this situation but, when you consider we were only trying to be good Samaritans, it makes you wonder how people can be so ungrateful and have such a lack of thought. I had eventually got the message and I knew that I had passed the point where I was going to put with it any longer. Fortunately, by this time (after living rent-free in my house for over a year) they had started to save for a deposit for a brand new house and, of course, we gave them whatever we could to set them up. I gave them a lot of my boxing prizes such as coffee tables, reading lamps, crockery and cutlery, and even sheets and blankets. In those days we used to box for those sort of prizes rather than trophies.

After my foster brother and his wife and baby moved out of our home we didn't hear from them for some time but eventually found out that they had lived in the new house for as long as they could without paying anything further on the mortgage.

They had left it to the point where they would be evicted from the property and the next thing I heard was that they had done a moonlight flit to Ireland. Everything we had lent or given to them was seized by the bailiffs. Of course, Sean being Sean, it wasn't long after he was back in Ireland that he got some good scams running that would make Del Boy Trotter in Only Fools and Horses look like a learner! After poor old Daisy died he got May, her sister, to sign the farm in Ireland over to him. He sold it for £6000, which was a snip for a place that was in such a beautiful position. A multi-millionaire from Dublin eventually built a mansion on the farm that would not have been out of place in the TV series Dallas. It just shows how things can change when you compare this with what the old farm used to be like and the way Daisy and May had to scrape a living in the tumbledown buildings. Let me make it clear that my foster brother didn't have to do anything illegal. He was educated and clever enough to have made a very good living, but I suppose he too was affected by the total lack of care that he had. He had also been ignored by the local officials and all those people who were responsible for looking after such problem families.

Although we'd solved a major problem when my foster brother moved out of our home to his new house there were more disruptions to come. They were the sort of thing you always fear but hope will never happen. On one awful night we got back home after a boxing tournament at the Grand Hotel in Leicester and I opened the front door to let Carol in. She went into the front room to put her things down while I went into the kitchen to put the kettle on and make some tea. It was then that I noticed that the back door was caved in. Carol had by then decided to go upstairs but I managed to stop her, rather abruptly and without giving her any explanation as to why I was acting in what must have seemed, to her, such an irrational manner. Of course, what had concerned me was that our uninvited visitor, or visitors, may still have been in the house. I had quickly realised that she might be in danger. I then made a thorough check of the rooms upstairs before allowing Carol to go further. No doubt she thought for a minute or two that I was a very ill mannered person. This was most certainly a terrible shock for Carol, and it made her so frightened that she could not bear to be in the house on her own after this. I was hoping that this would get better as time went on but she was determined that she would never be happy in the house again. The thief had only managed to steal a few pounds (the union dues that I collected from work) but they had taken so much more from us. Our feelings of happiness and security in the first home of our married life were gone.

So, apart from pinching the few pounds that were in the wardrobe there was a great deal more to come in terms of loss, and the big problem too was that the police had no idea where to look and where the blame lay in relation to the break in and theft. This plunged us into all the problems associated with buying another house and of moving. We came across the problem of being gazumped. There were a number of houses that we had looked at, and as far as we were concerned had done the deal on, only to find out several months down the road that somebody else had actually bought the house. We found the situation so distressing and frustrating that when we actually sold Fareham Avenue in Rugby we bought our bungalow in Shakespeare Gardens, also in

Rugby, without even looking at it. Also, it was a two bed-roomed property so we had actually come down from a three bed-roomed house. Such was the state of Carol's mind in wanting to get away from Fareham Avenue because of the experience of it being raided that we were desperate to move and didn't wait to count the costs.

Something else happened at this time that was to affect my life a lot but it wasn't something I had planned or really had any hand in – it was that old enemy destiny again. The Labour government of the time was wielding its axe in a Territorial Army shake up, which meant that it made it easier for Carol to persuade me to pack it in. She could still not bear to be on her own while I was away for two weeks at camp and she finally got her way.

Because of my boxing during this period I was known to all at Chrysler, where I was working, as Cas and it was at this time that 'Cas' put his foot in it good and proper with his good deed for the soup canteen. You will recall the soup incident mentioned earlier when I spilled the workers' soup in spectacular style. This soup was much appreciated by the operators in the cold factory during the winter months as working in there was like being in a sieve with the draughts that seemed to come from all directions. I am sure there will still be people who remember my misfortune when all that soup came cascading down the aisles of the Baginton plant and no doubt there has been many a smirk across their faces when their memories wander back to that fateful day.

That wasn't the only memorable incident there. We had a very sudden and untimely disruption to work at the packing CKD plant at Baginton in 1965. As the union representative, I had been around the plant and had seen the welding taking place and was always telling people connected with stores, including the superintendent, that the stillages were too high. One day I observed the same practice taking place, but worse than that they had the welders up in the roof doing some welding. The stillages could contain the full set of bits and pieces for cars and vans, most of which were being exported to Iran before the Ayatollah put his foot in it. But some of the stillages would contain the foam trim for the interiors of cars and vans. That foam was to be a deadly curse to the Baginton plant as it turned out to be the cause of the largest fire in the Midlands.

I was working in the plant on the morning of the fire and it is a day I will never forget. I saw that fire turn from a mere flicker to a raging inferno in seconds. It was a normal working day and I was making my way through the plant – the former Whitley Aircraft Works – to the Superintendent's office in the Goods Inwards Department to discuss some matters in my capacity as Shop Convenor. I don't know what made me look up to the ceiling as I walked between the stillages, stacked high on either side, but when I did, what I saw frightened me beyond belief. I saw a small flame run along the electric wires in the ceiling. It was like a train on a track. I found myself shouting along with lots of other workers to raise the alarm and then we were all running to get out. Running to save our lives. Hundreds of us stood outside and watched that building burn and there was nothing we could do. I felt weak at the thought of the sheer destruction I was witnessing and with the deep sadness as I realised that our lives would never be the same again. We were likely to be out of a job and people's lives were being changed as we looked helplessly on.

After the flames and fuss had died down and the danger to life and limb had passed, one of the side effects that I was left with was the anger I felt. The most annoying aspect was that I had repeatedly drawn attention to the ceiling and these stillages being stacked far higher than they should have been, but as often happened, no notice was taken. There was at that time an ongoing battle with union officials trying to penetrate some of the management's thinking when it came to safety. I know that sometimes the attention to 'Health and Safety' today could sometimes be said to have gone over the top, but the kind of safety that union officials like myself were trying to get across was simply common sense. Unfortunately, it would always be a battle with the management who seemed to be oblivious to this danger. For example, fire doors would be continuously blocked with stillages, packages or just-delivered materials. Although I would not claim that I was the most tidy person in the world, I do think that when it came to access to safety, and fire doors being unobstructed in case of an emergency that you had no control over, that I would be continuously alert. But no matter how many terrible disasters there had been prior to this fire, you can't always get your message across and people don't necessarily learn from mistakes. Catastrophes would still take place, whether in a commercial place like this or a dance hall for instance, and the consequences were always going to be very serious. Even if a bad fire such as this didn't cause death it disrupted many people's lives and some found themselves without work – all because of somebody's lack of attention to even the most obvious safety precautions.

But, to some people there were, even in the midst of that great devastation, some funny bits that people still remind me of. For example, during the months shortly before the fire there was always a shortage in the shops of some household needs such as toilet rolls, sugar and the like. These items periodically just disappeared from the shops and some ingenuity had to be used to keep the family supplied. Of course, a lot of people believed it was a big ploy by the manufacturers just to hike the prices up, as sometimes it was so difficult to get sugar, for example, that the price quadrupled. People were so happy just to get hold of a bit of sugar that they would pay the price and worry about the cost further down the road. In my case I just couldn't take a cup of tea without sugar so every opportunity I got when I was out, or attending meetings in Scotland and other places, I always made it my business to get a few pounds of sugar if I saw it in the shops, but I dared not take it home to Carol. She was so good-hearted that she would have given every grain of it away and left none for my tea, so I stored it in my locker at work. Now, at the time of the fire my locker was actually full to the brim with bags of sugar, but of course the fire had the lot. Out of all of the lockers in the line that were burned to a frazzle, it was obvious where Cas's locker stood because of the boost of extended fire which left a very definite mark which made it stand out from all the other lockers. A lot of my mates still talk about it today, 32 years later. It is still fresh in their minds – that sugar mountain in my locker all those years ago.

The fire left a great deal of uncertainty about our employment. There was a very hurried arrangement to move us to Stoke Aldermoor while they rebuilt the old plant and unfortunately, because of the lack of space and the numbers already employed at Stoke, not all of the people who were then employed at Baginton were able to be found work. It was done on the last in, first out basis. These touches of destiny can be life changing, and we lost a brilliant work area and the work we had put in to building the conditions that we had gained over the years went for nothing. It was nothing short of a disaster not just for the company, who lost a very valuable plant and a considerable amount of materials, but for all of those operators who had got the best working conditions that you could wish for and work that they enjoyed doing.

In the early years of our marriage Carol and I were lucky enough to be blessed with a growing, healthy family. As with all families, life did not always run smooth. Our second daughter, Mandy was one of the most awkward children that ever was born and most definitely did not believe in walking. She insisted on being pushed or carried everywhere she went. Debbie, our first child, never seemed to have that need to be carried around but she did have a problem, as a lot of children do, in carrying stuff around with her and she particularly liked taking my shoes or boots outside. Now, on one particular occasion, I had just bought a pair of new shoes as Carol had moaned so much about the state of my shoes that I had given in. Of course, with my background, I would always want to get the full wear out of everything, which was a real wind up to Carol who found it very hard to understand why I would insist on wearing shoes or clothes that were almost dropping to pieces. Before long I was hunting high and low for one of my new shoes and severely questioned poor little Debbie. It was so frustrating when something disappeared without any explanation and, of course, I focussed on Debbie because of her previous record in this department. She must have thought I had lost the plot as it turned out she had nothing to do with the shoe going down to the bottom of the street. It was that black dog from the bottom of Southey Road that had helped himself to my brand new shoe. This dog often paid us a visit and on this day he took a fancy to one of my shoes and took it away with him. You could have knocked me down with a feather when the owner of the dog turned up to say that he would pay for the damage. He was a good neighbour and had the honesty to own up to what had happened. But that is the sort of neighbours we have always had in Southey Road over the years. You could rely on them and depend on them. The poor innocent (on this occasion!) Debbie would have been about three years old then.

The bungalow on Southey Road (which we had bought without seeing) with two bedrooms, was starting to feel a bit small for us as the family was rapidly getting bigger. We had to start to focus on how we would overcome our space problems should we have any more children. I was being disappointed on a regular basis in terms of what sex the children were as I was hoping that after the first daughter we would have a boy. But that was not to happen. I came up with what I thought was the perfect solution to our lack of space and decided we would have a loft extension. Of course, I had a plan as to how to get it done as cheaply as possible. There was a Pack Development section at Chrysler in Baginton where they designed wooden cases for the ever-changing demand for case sizes from the customer. Sometimes there would be ten packs going out or sometimes there would be just one. The cases held vehicles that were in a complete knocked down state or they could contain spare parts for others that had previously supplied. In this department there was a horrific waste of money, manpower and materials as they would order dozens of cases of various sizes and at a stroke they would be rejected as they no longer came up to the specification when requirements changed – as they frequently did, so the wood used was no longer needed. A lot of people keen on a bit of DIY found this timber extremely useful for allotment sheds, tool sheds and various extensions that would be going on around some of their homes. But greed and corruption seemed to have its little fingerprints in such a development on a scale that you could never imagine and as the union representative I was asked to keep an eye on the situation. It was believed that some of the yard foremen were kind to many farmers in the area in terms of finding a home for these cases, so a lot of people, including my union members, asked me could I make sure that the kind deeds went to the workers at the plant rather than local farmers.

Keen to ensure fair play as always, I set about sorting this situation. I was assured by the then plant manager, Mr Wilpool, that the workers would get priority to any cases that were available as rejects. However, as in a lot of these situations some of the foremen in the yard would not have read the script (or if they had, they did not like it) and they continued to carry on as they saw fit and fairness didn't get a look in.

One afternoon I was approached by a fork lift truck driver in the yard. He and his mate wanted some cases. I think they were going in for keeping hens. This put the idea into my head that maybe these cases might be handy for making a loft conversion at our home. The foreman told me, well if you want those cases you can have them on the condition that they go before five o'clock that evening. I suppose he thought he was being clever and that this task was too big to carry out in the time he'd allotted. What he didn't know was that the truck driver had already said that he had found an artic lorry and driver that would take these cases to the three drops in Rugby for himself, his mate and me. So far, so good, but sometimes when fellows decide that they are going to do things they haven't fully consulted with their good ladies and it has a tendency to come back and bite where it gives the most grief. Later that evening, Carol looked out of the front window as the light had completely gone and to her amazement she saw the lorry the length of the road and as high as the lampposts outside. She turned to me and asked what has he stopped here for, you said you were having a few cases but there is a mountain on there. Hurriedly looking out of the window at the monster lorry I told her not to worry as I wasn't having all the cases – my two mates were having some as well. This didn't satisfy Carol, of course. She didn't seem too convinced and she seemed very edgy. The best way I could describe her was that she was like the children's cartoon character Zebedee, as she was rushing aimlessly in all directions just like he did. The artic lorry parked in our street was blocking the full length of the road, which luckily didn't cause too much of a problem traffic-wise as you could go all around and come into the street from the other end. The load on the lorry did cause us a problem though as we didn't have a forklift to get the stuff off the lorry, which meant my portion would all have to be manhandled off. As always in my little escapades, there was worse to come.

One of the mates sharing this load, Maurice, was always longing for this type of timber to make things as he was very good with the saw, but I think his wife, Audrey, had a hand in his decision to cancel his share of this timber. Yes, you have guessed, I have now ended up with a double helping of this mammoth load that was blocking out the sun as it waited outside our little bungalow.

I am afraid that when we had finished unloading my original share, and the unwanted portion as well, the whole garden was packed out with not an inch to spare. Worse than that, Carol couldn't get to the washing line. Of course, with women if things go exactly as they want it then it tends to be a totally unacceptable situation. But this particular situation was going to take some time to resolve and I hadn't yet hit on a plan to sort it out. But I have to say that Carol had great resilience on this occasion and decided drastic action should be taken. She announced that she would go to all the houses in Southey Road offering timber just as long as they collected it; no money necessary. Now, you might think this was an empty threat aimed at getting me to take swift action but maybe you haven't fully appreciated the strength of character of this girl I had married. When I came home from work the following evening, I was met by a steady stream of people coming down Southey Road carrying wood in all manner of transport. Some had sack barrows, wheelbarrows, and even prams. You would be amazed how in just a few days they started to make a big hole in all this lovely plywood – the finest timber. Some people made rabbit hutches or tool sheds and there were garage extensions, or allotment sheds springing up in the neighbourhood. It was impressive to see what they turned their timber in to, and some of this work is still there to this day.

Of course, all this put a damper on my doing the extension in the loft. Carol convinced me that I had better be realistic as to what could be done and if we were to have an extension then I would be better advised to get a loft conversion company to do it and that, of course, is what I did. Although the problems were receding in the garden, there was yet more fun in store relating to the timber at Chrysler, even though by this time I had heard more than enough about it and would have been happy never to see any more timber from the Packing Department. The superintendent for the Parts Inwards section was involved with the committee for the Coventry Carnival and he had arranged for them to have what timber they needed to make a Norman-type castle complete with drawbridge, chains, lookout, the lot. It was a very impressive affair. After the Carnival he came to me and asked if I could find a home for the castle. As you can see, people didn't just come to me with union problems at work; I was starting to get all sorts of problems to resolve. Sometimes I resolved these problems very quickly and sometimes they took longer. On this occasion, I decided that the castle would be ideal as a play area for my children. We were expecting our third child and I thought that having the castle might turn out useful for the children, but it took a lot of persuasion to get Carol to accept my latest hair-brained idea. Of course, I always kept her on her toes and she would never know what was coming next, but maybe you have guessed it – another artic lorry turned up with the superintendent's problem castle on board! This now needed to be offloaded and erected at the bottom of our garden, much to my next door neighbour's horror. But at least it wasn't interfering with the washing line, so Carol could get her washing out and life could carry on as normal. In all these sort of Alice in Wonderland-inspired antics, destiny has its own part to play and although this might have seemed like one of my sillier schemes, this turned out well in the end. The castle kept the children fully occupied as a den area and play area which could have been described as a 'children's nest'. If you poked it as you might poke an ant's nest children of all shapes and sizes would be crawling through gateways, draw-bridges and lookouts. That castle was a place of fun for many years.

Some people seem to find it easier and more convenient to let their children wander off and play with other people's children but I took a different view. I was happy to know my children were in our own back garden. It gave us a better chance of knowing what they were up to. While the children were growing up there was never an empty second. I even kept some hens in the garden for them. They had the dogs, Toby and Rover, guinea pigs and rabbits. They had one particular black and white rabbit that everybody was moaning about because they reckoned it bit them. I couldn't see this myself as I had actually never come across a tame rabbit being like that. But one day I got a shock when I was giving the cage a quick clean out and suddenly found that he was hanging onto my little finger! It is funny, under these circumstances, how quickly you become converted and you are telling the children to keep their fingers away from the rabbit's mouth.

When we got a really nice day we would go to Daventry to the open-air swimming pool. As the girls had so many friends who regularly spent their days in our garden this would create a lot of arguments as to who was going to be able to come. (I am now meeting people forty-odd years later reminding me of these events and some feel quite put out that I don't remember them.) In those days I had a little 1300 Morris and I would have to say the way we packed that car I could have been in competition with the canners trying to get sardines into a tin. I often lost count of how many children were actually in the car – they were all sizes and ages, in the boot and everywhere. It's a good job that we didn't have things like seat belts and restrictions on numbers in cars that we have today because there would have been a lot of disappointed children. What a disaster it would have been if they could not be in the party going to the swimming pool where everyone had a brilliant time. Thinking about it, I suppose some of these new regulations have helped in terms of safety but I think any responsible person whose car was loaded up with children would drive accordingly. Today they have their straps, chairs and smaller numbers but they are all going as if they are trying to win a race at Brands Hatch, so the advantage of not having these overloaded cars has been diluted.

Life was certainly good at this point. The years at Baginton were some of the best years of my life in every respect. Not only was my family happy, healthy and growing in number, but I had gained respect as a trade union leader, as an organiser, as a boxing promoter and matchmaker, and also gained respect as an active boxer. I know how very lucky I have been in my life. When I look over my shoulder and think of my beginnings it is hard to believe that a person who was so suppressed and so denied of any civilised communication amongst his fellow beings could have made a life like I have. The frustration of being uneducated can be like water by the sea, it laps up around your ankles and in the end many a poor soul is totally submerged by the lack of education. Many people from poor backgrounds and without the necessary start in life have become victims of alcohol abuse, drug abuse and in some cases have become involved in very serious crime, because these people would have been so frustrated. In some cases these people would have been far cleverer than a good many who were their bosses, and it was only because they did not have the education that they were being prevented from being promoted into management and so on. That is the sort of problem that can lead to hang-ups that can drive people to despair. I suppose I was lucky that I found a great wife and that I was submerged in amateur boxing and the trade union movement.

As I say, my family was expanding during the 70s and we soon had our third daughter, Gail. I would come back from Harborough Magna Maternity Hospital to tell everybody, yet again, the disappointment of having another girl. You would think after the third time you would get used to it, but believe me I was shocked. I helped the nurse at the birth of my fourth and final daughter, Kerry, when her birth proved a bit difficult. The lack of a son is something I can't change though, so that is what I am going to have to put up with whether I like it or not. I suppose you could say I was the most unsuitable person to bring up girls, as I could not cope easily with their prim and proper ideas and their fancy clothing requirements. For me, this part was always going to be a nightmare but we are all still here!

Chapter 14

Survival

Many, many times in the years since I came to England, and certainly now as I write this book and look back on my wonderful life with all its blessings, I wonder how I survived my early years when many others did not. It wasn't just the ones who died – maybe they were the lucky ones. There most certainly weren't many children born in the Bethany Home where I started my life who were not affected for life in some way or another because of that experience. As readers of my first book, Hannah's Shame, will be aware, the total lack of care that the children who had the misfortune to stay there were subjected to is something for which, I believe, the Irish Government is responsible.

Because of the research that I had to do for my first book, I have had to bite the bullet and realise that the Ireland I love was ruled by people who were not the Christians they professed to be. When I uncovered for myself how they treated children it was so hard to take. These were innocent children remember – some born out of wedlock, or children who were simply just not wanted, even by some people who were married. I discovered that sectarian nonsense took place and prevailed where one religion was trying to engineer their numbers on their side. Now, it would not have been so bad if these religious organisations were taking the children from one religious order to another to give them a better life and better care, but of course that wasn't what was important to these religion-mad people who seemed to have gone over the top from 1922 onwards. This total lack of concern for the wellbeing of the children placed in their care carried on for decades – certainly until the late 60s. They disregarded children's identities and shipped them to any part of the world who would have them, and some were even sold to Americans for as much as they could get. There was never any interest in finding out if these people were fit to have the children. And all of this was done in the name of God!

At one point, they even had Archbishop McDaid sitting with the Ministers of Education and Health determining the fate of those unwanted children, and they showed no consideration whatsoever for their well being. Of course he would have been quite happy to simply see the non-Catholics wiped out. People of the Catholic religion were not the only ones to blame in this awful situation. We had the same approach from the Protestants, who were scurrying around giving these unwanted children to any family, or organisation, who were prepared to take them and who were prepared to raise them as Protestants. This is what happened to me. Because of this grotesque, inhuman, un-Christian act to humanity, a great many of these unwanted children simply died before they reached the age of five because of the dreadful way they were treated. As I say, I was so lucky to survive.

One of the homes that featured in this sectarian battle was the Bethany Home. I cannot speak in any detail about the other homes; I am only covering the home I was in, which was the Bethany Home in Rathgar, Dublin 6. I suppose some people, and particularly a lot of Irish people, would like to say 'sure, that was the way things were then and just get on with your life and forget about it'. Maybe for people who have not been through this experience that would be their way of dealing with it, but I take the view, rightly or wrongly, that for the vast majority of these children who died before the age of five, through such grotesque lack of care, it would have been impossible for them to ignore their treatment. It is certainly impossible for me to ignore my experiences and all I have found out about the situation since. I believe that the people who were lucky enough to have survived that ordeal have a duty to bring it into the light and uncover the darkness that has surrounded these innocent souls. The victims were simply children who had done nobody any wrong and their only wrong was to have arrived unplanned on this earth. I feel a responsibility to expose and denounce the horrific conditions in which they died through lack of the most basic human care. Their deaths should never be sealed away without people knowing about them. In addition to the exposure of these wrongs, I believe there should be a monument so that nobody could ever forget what took place in establishments like the Bethany Home. This should be a lantern for all children to throw light on their existence, irrespective of whether they were planned, wanted, or otherwise so that what happened to them could never happen again.

As I grew up in Ireland I never had the slightest idea that my country could be so hysterically mad and inhuman in dealing with this type of problem. In my research as I go on I get some surprises that I didn't bargain for and the judgement of the Irish Government has been called into question over and over again. I didn't know before I started digging, for example, that a book with the slightest hint of sexuality interwoven in the stories could be deemed unsuitable and that you were not allowed to sell it in the Free State of Eire. Who did these people think they were to decide what you could read and what you could not? Of course, ignorant people like me would have thought automatically that it was somewhere like Russia that would dictate this sort of dogma, or the nonelected dictatorship of a banana state, but I discovered that one author in Ireland wrote twenty books and was not allowed to even see one of them. It is beyond belief. I have to pinch myself to think that I believed I belonged to a free country but found that it was one of the most sectarian, and also one of the most literary controlled states, on earth. Believe me, it doesn't give me any pride to have to face up to what took place in Ireland prior to the 1990s and it is with great shame that I have to reflect upon it. Painful as it may be, I know that if you don't reflect on these things, and instead accept it as it was, you don't learn not to make those mistakes again. I've thought long and hard about what could possibly have brought my country to this state. I suppose when you consider that people in Irish society and politics dripped of sectarianism it is no surprise that the society created inflicted upon the state of Ireland the conditions that brought about this horrendous nightmare that has now been uncovered in relation to unwanted children and children born outside of wedlock. When you add this to the fact that Catholic bishops insisted that if a Catholic parent was involved with an out of marriage child, that child would have to be raised as a Catholic with the other parent having no say in the matter, then if that isn't Bin Ladenism I don't know what is. Couldn't so-called Christians have considered the wellbeing of the child rather than just being intent on spreading their religious dogma?

These people should hang their heads in shame. They may think that they got the Celtic Tiger because they had to ship the majority of the people out of the country, who in turn had to send home money to keep their relatives alive. In truth, the Celtic Tiger was a hard fought battle and there were millions of Irish people who had to pay the price for that to come about. Of course, there are many people living in a sort of Utopia in Ireland. They don't like to have to wake up and smell the coffee and take reality on board. They should be ashamed that they do not yet have to go out of Ireland to do charitable work. The sad truth is that there is an awful lot of charity work needed in every city and town in Ireland in relation to unwanted children and young people. Keep your eye on it; it hasn't gone away.

I am still fighting my long battle for justice with the Irish Government in relation to the 2002 Redress Bill and the thorny issue of the non-Catholic homes, (such as the Bethany Home in Rathgar, Co. Dublin, where I was) being left out of this arrangement. The state brought in the Redress Bill to compensate the children who were betrayed by government agencies but, of course, this only included Catholic-run homes. They completely overlooked the non-Catholic homes. It wasn't just Protestant children affected by this – there were far more 'half and half' religion born babies in the Bethany Home than there ever were Protestants so the fact that Catholics were involved appears to have been overlooked. A huge number of unmarried mothers and their babies came from the north of Ireland, particularly during the war years when there was a high number of troops in Northern Ireland. Before the war some people went to England to have illegal abortions but the majority headed for Dublin to have their children. What the Irish Government didn't do in 2002 was to make any provisions for the likelihood of there being a problem with the non-Catholic population of Ireland, and I suppose the best way of expressing the religious divide, certainly in the 1950s, was likening them to the Jews in Britain, or the Asians – that is to say they lived in the country but they weren't taken very seriously. For example, if you wanted school records from the Church of Ireland national schools, from the Government archives, you would be unable to get them. The reason for this was because they never kept any. That is how much of a priority we were, (or were not) as far as the Irish state was concerned. So when this 2002 Agreement came about they sailed straight down the line without consideration for the non-Catholics. Out of hundreds of non-Catholic homes they included just two and because of their embarrassment they added another three homes in their last list of 13 homes. These have finally been included in the Redress Bill because of the involvement of part-Catholic children. When Dr Woods, then Minister of Education, was negotiating with the Catholic Church regarding this problem it was realised that some of the children from these other homes were not pure Protestants. They were 'half and half' which meant, in some cases, that they actually went to places like the Artane concentration camps (known officially as Artane Industrial School) after they left the other junior homes.

Leaving non-Catholics out of the Redress arrangements was surely a mistake of the highest order and it beggars belief that highly paid government officials, lawyers, supposed experts and religious leaders could all have got together and still made this grave error. But the more I uncover as I do my research, the more I realise that this is, in fact, the case. They've got it wrong. I have no doubts whatever that Protestants born in the south of Ireland class themselves as Irish nationals and under the Constitution of Ireland anyone born within its jurisdiction is to be treated exactly the same, irrespective of what religion, colour, or otherwise they are. People born in Ireland free state were Irish citizens irrespective of religion. This is also covered by the 1908 Children's Act which states that all children have got to be treated equally by the state. But the Redress Bill flies in the face of this belief.

When I researched my background and met members of my mother's family I was to discover that the real tragedy of my childhood wasn't just the poverty and the hunger or the lack of decent clothing, it was the total absence of love and affection. What I had really missed out on was having a family who cared. You would have thought that uncovering this lack of care to get to where I was with my first book was bad, but I must admit that after finally getting hold of the 101 documents that the Irish Government have denied existed for ten years was a shock even for me. These documents were

only released to me after years of perseverance and no wonder they wanted to hide the
details. It can only fill any decent human
being with horror to think that all that
happened in my childhood happened in
their own life time in Ireland. As I sifted
through this mountain of paperwork, I
could not believe the things I was learning
about my childhood. There were Inspectors'
Reports from the Bethany Home, corres-
pondence between departments in both
local and national government – and it was
all shocking. I found out for example, that I
had been near death as an infant when I
contracted the contagious disease of Per-
tussus. This leaves the sufferer with flu-like
symptoms that can last for the rest of their
life. This explained a health problem for me,
but annoyed me intensely that such essen-
tial information had been hidden from me
for so long. The over-riding feeling I was left
with when I had gone through this paperwork was shock at just how sectarian my
country was. It certainly brings you up with
a jolt when you find all this out, but I now
know that this is only the tip of the iceberg
as to what is in the archives. The odd thing
about all of this is that it had taken me a
lifetime to realise that this is the way it was,

and here I am, still fighting the Ministry of Education, the Minister for Health & Children, and the Minister for Justice. All of their efforts to date have been to frustrate me and to inform me that I didn't exist and that this was borne out as far as the 1908 Children's Act was concerned. This Act was brought in by Britain to protect all children of all religious persuasions but was not there, in my case, to protect me, a non-Catholic child. But, of course, I now have the records, the results of the research that has taken a lifetime. These documents make the case very clear that the 1908 Children's Act, when implemented by the State, was always done for the benefit of Catholic children only. I have no doubt now that had there been a war involving Eire from 1922 the Minister for Education and the Health Board would have been on trial for war crimes against children.

I can't make this point about the treatment of children clear enough, and I would never be able to express the horrors that babies, infants and children had to endure. And the Minister in charge, who knew at all levels what was going on, did nothing. We have all seen the horrendous footage on TV of the

Belgian Congo, Albania and Bosnia, and the Eastern Bloc countries of how they treated their unwanted children, but I never realised that my own country was part of that same horror machine. These people will never be able to walk tall until they are able to face up to their responsibilities from the past. They have a duty to all the children who have died and all of the ones left wounded through their gross miscarriage of justice. They drew their big, fat salaries and lived their twilight days on a very nice pension, but there cannot ever be peace within Ireland's own heart until they recognise that they have their own skeletons in their own cupboards that need to be dealt with.

I know that a lot of Irish people will jump to the defensive position and use the arguments as an excuse for what has happened. They might, understandably, say 'Wasn't it a very impoverished period of time? Wasn't everyone very poor in those days?' It would be nice if it was as simple as that explanation, but of course it is not. The suffering that happened to a lot of children in Ireland, particularly the non-Catholics, had nothing to do with poverty but it has everything to do with dogma. They may try and use those sorts of explanations for them to find a comfort zone, but I am afraid my research explodes that myth. Most of the children born in the Bethany Home, Rathgar, Dublin, were from some of the best of families in Ireland and yet they were sentenced to total poverty, total neglect and total abuse by society. I would like to know why the Red Cross, during the war and after, would not accept taking refugee kids from these homes run by the church, irrespective of what religion they were. Unbelievable abuse and neglect of the most vulnerable people in society took place and yet it did not cause the people who had the responsibility to protect these kids to blink an eye. They obviously quite happily accepted these conditions.

The people in authority treated unplanned pregnancies as if they didn't exist. But, of course, Dublin was flooded with unwanted pregnancies from the north of Ireland which, due to the movements of troops, went off the scale. This was added to the unplanned pregnancies – such as my mother's – that the girls of Eire had to contend with. Because of the war years many of these unfortunate girls were unable to make the trip to the UK to have illegal abortions and this added to the problems at this time.

Of course the non-Catholics, who were complaining bitterly to the Irish Government for help, were most anxious to pretend that this was not happening and in my opinion it gave the Irish Government officials dealing with these matters a stick to hit the opposite side of religion over the head with. The Catholic authorities wanted them to break cover and publicly accept the glare of ridicule that this was happening in their community as well as the Catholic community. But, of course, it was brinkmanship to the very line because the Irish officials would wish to eat broken glass before they would admit that they had such a huge problem. So, instead of being embarrassed by the reality of the situation and doing something about it, they fought in darkness with the Irish Government to get help and simply allowed the kids to actually rot in their nappies. It wasn't what they physically did to these infants that was so horrifyingly wrong in my eyes, it was the fact that they knew what was happening and allowed it to continue in silence to the point where a great many of the children died before they were five years old, and most of the others who survived had health problems that would never let them forget the lack of care they got in the children's homes. It is Ireland's shame and a true tragedy for the children caught up in the petty arguments and lack of care.

No doubt these situations involving unwanted children are not only in Ireland. They must have happened in other countries too, but I can only talk with any authority about what happened in Ireland at this stage, as that is what affected me. My research – and my fight – goes on and I am now getting e-mails and letters from all around Ireland and the UK, and there is interest being shown in the United States of America and Canada following the publication of my first book, 'Hannah's Shame'. It is amazing how so many people are able to relate to the experiences that are covered in the book, and how some of them now are able to take comfort after reading it to assist their own lives They have even told me how proud they are that I have taken the time to record the events. It made me realise how deeply affected some of these people still are 60 and 70 years after the event. In Wicklow town, in the little bookshop there, they have sold around two hundred copies of 'Hannah's Shame' and people who have read it have named it the 'lovely little book'.

Can you imagine what pride and self-satisfaction the feedback on my first book has given me? To think that these people feel that it can help them and others, and that it can help all unwanted children of yesterday, today and tomorrow. Who could have believed that a wretched kid running around the Wicklow hills in rags, who never knew the love of his mother and father, or any of his blood relations, who left school at the age of thirteen years, unable to read or write, could have ever written a book that his now ploughing a furrow so deep and so straight. As Canon Baird, who I knew in my childhood and managed to make contact with after I'd written my first book, has said to me, if anyone was leaving a memorial behind after their life he couldn't think of a more fitting memorial than the book 'Hannah's Shame'. When someone like that, who is a learned person, made comments such as those to me, a most definitely non-learned person, it made me feel very humble indeed. It made me think of the more important things in life and how lucky I have been as I pass through to the next world. I suppose writing a book would be the last thing in this world that you could ever connect me with. Now it is truly astonishing when I read comments and reviews on Internet websites across the world, and review critics giving my book four or five stars. I know that had they given me just one star out of five they would not have needed to have given me any more as even that would have surpassed my wildest dreams.

I often wonder now what would poor old Daisy and May, and my foster father think as to how things have unfolded for the 'poor idiot', as I was referred to growing up. Would they ever have believed that one day I would have a book registered on the British library system and that the Dublin library system would have twelve copies of my book in their social history section. I suppose there are an awful lot of people who have got university qualifications and so on, and some of them with lifetime dreams of publishing their own book, but they have never achieved it. But I've done it – and now I'm on my way to doing it a second time. I suppose some people might think, God you are going on a bit about this but if these same people had experienced the same start as I had they most certainly would say that I couldn't go on enough about it.

Of course, I have spent many hours looking for answers to insoluble questions. I often wonder why was I born to a mother who had only one interest, and that was in herself and the snobbery she and her family were submerged in. I have often wondered too why was I in a religion that was so snobby and had so little to do with Christianity. I wonder why I was born in a country that was submerged in fundamentalists that it would make even the Asians feel jealous. Over the years many people have tried to answer these questions for me with some very interesting – and sometimes just plain daft – suggestions. I was interviewed recently on Wexford radio where an offspring of one of the very wealthy families that I was brought up among phoned in and left a number for me to ring him. I did this and he told me he believed the reasons why my foster father wasn't helped by the local dignitaries and officers of the Church of Ireland was because they felt he did not do enough to help himself. I suppose there is some merit in the point made, but isn't it making it very complicated when you have make the change from being a simple good Samaritan to becoming a judge and jury over this unbelievable plight of a family. Would there not have been a more important point about what a father of three children was? Could it not have been that whatever he did or didn't do, it could not have been right to punish three helpless kids by saying that people like my foster father weren't doing enough to help themselves. I suppose this is the Church of Ireland's 'pull up your socks, and a good soldier never looks back' attitude but in my opinion this is where they become so submerged in their own importance that they are unable to recognise that there were children in desperate need of care and attention and a need to be fulfilled that real Christian behaviour would deal with. Probably when they came to those conclusions that my foster father didn't do enough to help himself it made them able to live with their own conscience, whilst the problem within their midst could be blurred and put into a cocoon which spins out of sight and out of mind. So, what I have to say in reply to the point made is I am sorry Mr Offspring of those big wigs in that little parish in

Ireland. That was not the correct answer to this particular problem. You need to go back to the drawing board and come up with a better answer than that. At the end of the day, the families who were around my foster father at that time, including the vicar of the parish, do have a share of the guilt and shame that cannot be argued against. They simply have to bite the bullet and accept that what happened was wrong, and I will take a lot of convincing before I can ever alter my posture in regard to this matter.

My first book 'Hannah's Shame' was called that because of the shame that sank into every part of the society, including my mother's own shame, my shame and the shame of her family. A lot more people have got to have shame regarding these sorts of situations than just the people who have to live with the effects of the lack of humanity and the lack of differences that could have been made by society and their own neighbours. Of course, it is very hard to have to accept blame when it is not your blame. My mother has to accept her blame. Although the Church of Ireland, the government of the day, and some of the Church of Ireland families could have made a difference they didn't. That is also their shame.

I will continue to push for recognition of the Bethany Home under the Redress Bill and I will, as ever, continue to fight the personal demons left behind by my upbringing.

Chapter 15

Finding out who I am

When researching for my first book, 'Hannah's Shame', I came across a very helpful historian, from Wicklow town. He very kindly sent me some priceless photographs and information about my social background and history in the district and country that I grew up in. One of the photographs he sent me was from the Barndarrigh School showing a group of children and their priest. When I looked at the picture after all those years I thought to myself the parents of those boys could be so proud. You could only have immense respect for them and their society who had turned them out so smartly for their school. When I think of the rags that I wore to Dunganstown School I was part of one poor family in that parish but in the Catholic parish of Barndarrigh there would have been dozens of extremely poor families. You can say what you like; the Barndarrigh School's society took their responsibilities a great deal more seriously than did the Dunganstown society, which were Church of Ireland. This historian also told me an amusing story of how Wicklow got its name. It is said that St Patrick was in the area and asked the people of the area to help him find something to eat. They then caught a stray dog, skinned it and cooked it for him instead of giving up one of their precious sheep. When St Patrick discovered their deception, he called them a 'wicked, low people'.

I have struggled for my entire life to come to terms with the start in life I had. Probably for well educated and balanced young people, many of the things I have had problems with would not have seemed so important. But, taking into account the suffering and neglect that people like me went through, the picture has become clearer as time has passed. I suppose it is always difficult to have to accept the truth because you never really want to believe that you were so deprived as an individual. The fact is that I was in an even worse position, growing up in Ireland and working for farmers, than a coloured slave boy would have been in terms of somebody looking out for me or governments trying to protect me. The poor, white, Irish 'slave boy' would have been far more useful to their employers than a coloured boy because the coloured boys were snatched from loving families who cared about them, whereas the white Irish slave boy was unwanted and unloved by anybody so he was likely to work harder – and longer.

It may surprise some people that this whole thing happened within living memory, but you have to accept the reality of the situation and, as they say, wake up and smell the coffee. Unwanted children like me had to endure all this so it is no good pretending it did not happen, pussyfooting around the subject as the Irish would love to do – they loved to pretend everything in the garden was rosy when in fact there wasn't a God damned rose in the garden, but that seems to be the nature of Irish people. Of course, over the latter years the Irish people have become more aware of their real Ireland and the goings on in society than they would ever have dreamt of in earlier years. I have reflected long and hard on the effect all this has had on me, of course, and I know the affects have run throughout my life. It was a big step jumping from a slavery situation to freedom of sorts and even that had its problems because, in some cases, you can go over the top in being the little rebel. The odd thing is you are, as a person, totally unaware of all this mayhem running through your mind and it is many, many years before you can accept things and be brave enough to put your hands up and surrender to your real past and, more importantly, deal with it. The situation I found myself in and which was my life as a boy and youth growing up in Ireland was like an octopus. It had so many tentacles that could reach out and touch every part of your life, whether it was to do with working or whether it was to do with socialising for example, so the repercussions go on and on. But still my love of Ireland and Dunganstown, Co. Wicklow, was never in any way questioned. I was so naïve, even when I came to England in the early sixties I didn't realise that the society in which I was raised was a long way from being civilised in its attitude to the unwanted. I don't know whether it is because of an inbuilt denial that we dare not allow our thoughts to wander into whether our state or our church could be at fault, but we seem to refuse to recognise where the fault lay.

The Catholics have had an apology from Mr Ahern, the former Taoiseach of Ireland for the things that went on while children were in government care. The non-Catholics are still waiting for their apologies. It is important to remember that there is no organisation, governmental or non-governmental, that represents the minority religious organisations in Ireland. These non-Catholics had the same abuse, neglect and shameful experiences as others – but no apology as yet. We know there have been a few exceptions to non-Catholics being included in the Redress Bill of 2002 but, of course, for the majority of non-Catholics there has been no progress whatsoever. I have found that it is very difficult in the Irish Free State to get exposure regarding this shameful episode in Irish history from the national media – TV, radio or newspapers – and anything you do get is like extracting teeth. However, I do have to say that some of the small provincial newspapers and radio stations have been like a breath of fresh air with their fairness.

Despite my growing doubts about the situation in Ireland, I still kept my connections with the old country. Of course, my foster family in Ireland was the only family that I knew and I would visit my aunts Daisy and May and my foster father as a duty. For me not to do it would be somehow shameful, sinful and totally unacceptable to my character. I remember one of these trips in particular. After I brought my brand new mini I decided to drive to Liverpool to get the boat over to Ireland to visit my foster father and Daisy and May. In those days they didn't have the drive-on ferries, (or at least if they did I knew nothing about them). On the boats in those days there used to be a big, rope, net-like sling that they would put around the cars and then the crane on the dockside would lower them into position and they would be parked accordingly. I shall never forget the first trip that I made, as the dock men loading my car were none too bothered in how they swung it around and if it bumped into pillars on its way down it would not cost them a thought. I was not too happy about them treating my beloved mini like that, I can tell you. My mini was one of the first cars loaded on that particular crossing and I assumed, wrongly, that I would have been the first off. Unfortunately for me not only was I the very last to come off, but as my car was hoisted by the crane, which looked a great distance from the deck of the ship, the dock men on the other side in Dublin North Wall were not too happy about their working conditions and everything stopped. When I made enquiries as to why my car was left aloft, swinging in the wind, I was informed that the dockers had gone to a union meeting. Of course, my union connections made me very aware that union decisions can be very disruptive to the lives of other people and this incident certainly influenced my thinking throughout the years that followed when I was involved in union negotiations.

When I eventually got my mini landed, it was brilliant driving it to Dunganstown, Co. Wicklow. Although I was born in Dublin I will never know how I drove from Dublin to Dunganstown, as Dublin is one of the maddest places I have ever had the misfortune of driving in. It was a chaotic and frightening experience. I tried to keep a cool head and prayed that I did not get to look like the other cars that were passing by me with big chunks out of them. I got to the cart road to the Hill House and then I had to negotiate the dirt track, which was not an easy thing to do with a vehicle with mini wheels, because of all the enormous ruts. Nevertheless it was still good to be able to park in the yard at the Hill House and get my foster father and aunts Daisy and May out to inspect the car. I don't know about them, but I was very proud. I think they thought that they had seen the impossible; the 'poor eejit', as I was referred to when growing up, had accomplished what I had.

But old habits don't change easily, and particularly with Daisy. She was never shy in coming forward. She was quick to ask 'Derry can you go to Coles?' They never called me Derek, always Derry. 'Would you go to Coles and get a few things' and, of course, the fire wasn't going to be forgotten either. On the shopping list for me was an item I had never seen while I was in Ireland. They were things called briquettes which were a manufactured way of dealing with the old-fashioned turf pieces. Since I was paying for the shopping on this occasion there would be nobody looking for sticks to burn like we did when I was a child. It is strange that when I smelled the turf burning it brought back all of the memories of my deprived childhood and made me wonder how I ever survived it. I enjoyed my trips to Ireland to see these old foster relatives but I suppose people who have read my first book, 'Hannah's Shame', would have difficulty in understanding how I could have had any love or respect for my foster family. I will never know all of the answers, all that I do know is that they were the only people in my young life that I knew as a family, and I had no problem in helping them in any way that I could. In fact I would have felt a complete failure, a betrayer of humanity, had I not responded in the way that I did.

On the trip to Ireland in my mini I took the aunts Daisy and May, and my foster father, to Glendalough to the seven churches, one of the most beautiful places on earth. Although it was not very far away from where they lived it would have been very rarely that they ever actually went there so it was a treat for all of us. Glendalough is where they had the round towers, which were there prior to gunpowder advances in scientific methods in destroying property, and churches and monasteries would have the lookouts there and be able to see the invaders heading for their treasures. They would pull up the ladders and would have enough food and stocks to last for many months until the invaders gave up.

All that area of Co. Wicklow, right through to Newtown Mount Kennedy, would have been part of the Fitzgerald family estate going back to the 10th century, and then it became Lord Leinster's estate, which had connections with the city of Leicester in England. I heard that one of the Lord Leinsters of fairly recent times would have been seen regularly in his regalia as he often wore it in his garden and around the house. Of course, I have no idea whether Lord Leinster was in any way connected with my family in Ireland as I was far too busy researching the Linster's, Foy's and Doyles. As readers of my first book may recall, Foy was my mother's maiden name and Doyle was my father's family name. Unfortunately, I had picked the wrong horse and now I needed to go back to the drawing board regarding the history of the family name of Leinster. I learned that although there are a lot of people going around who were Leinsters, they were unaware that they were, in fact, Linsters. Some of these mistakes were deliberately done, particularly if they were to do with the Crown forces, and others were caused through ignorance in regard to the incorrect spelling of the name.

On each of my trips to Ireland over the years I managed to fit in a bit of research into my family name and background. I saw lots of places on these trips, especially in my own county, Wicklow, where I was raised, that I did not know existed even though a lot of these areas and places are within a twenty mile radius of where I grew up. Because of the lack of means of transport you tended not to wander too far as you had enough walking to do in every day life without walking for pleasure. What my trips did give me – apart from lots of information about my background and frustration with the system that put me in the awful position I was in as a child – was just how beautiful my country is. This, to me makes it even more of a tragedy that the government and authorities can't get it right in terms of admitting, and putting right, their mistakes.

But after all this misery and frustration that I have endured – and I'm sure some of you must be saying what a miserable bloke and an awful life – I have to say that I feel so lucky. I'm lucky to have found such a wonderful woman to share my life and to have produced four lovely daughters who have blessed us with nine grandchildren. Yes, it may have been a life that was indeed miserable in parts but I have never, ever, been unhappy in myself. I remember my Aunts Daisy and May saying many times 'Count your blessings, count them one by one' – and I've got a lot of blessings in my life. An unexpected blessing at this stage in my life has been my books. Writing them has turned into a journey that I could never have predicted. I feel that all the people who read my first book and contacted me to tell me how it made them feel have become my friends. These friends have accompanied me on a long and sometimes difficult but always hopeful journey and I would like to thank them. Their appreciation and understanding shows me the strength of humanity and makes me feel humble. Producing my books has been a remarkable experience and one that I hope to continue with another chapter of my life but, for now, I think I need a little break and a cup of tea. Then I'll have time to ponder some more.

Thank you all.

The publishers hope that this book has given you enjoyable reading. Large Print Books are especially designed to be as easy to see and hold as possible. If you wish a complete list of our books please ask at your local library or write directly to:

Magna Large Print Books
Magna House, Long Preston,
Skipton, North Yorkshire.
BD23 4ND

This Large Print Book, for people
who cannot read normal print,
is published under the auspices of

THE ULVERSCROFT FOUNDATION